C000172163

METRObUS

The Company's First Ten Years

Andrew Boag

Capital Transport

First published 1994

ISBN 185414 159 7

Published in association with Metrobus Ltd
by Capital Transport Publishing
38 Long Elmes, Harrow Weald, Middlesex

Printed by The KPC Group, Ashford, Kent

© Andrew Boag 1994

Front Cover
Route 357 was the first service operated by Metrobus in 1983. Ten years later, Leyland
Olympian K816 HMV pulls away from Orpington Station, bound for Croydon. *Mike Harris*

Back cover
Dennis Dart J707 EMX approaches the village of Downe on route 146 with Holwood House in
the background. *Graham Sanders*

Contents

AEC Reliance ODV 405W is the only original vehicle which remains in the Metrobus fleet. It is seen here pausing during an afternoon tour at Northiam in Sussex in April 1989. *Graham Sanders*

Preface

This book sets out to document the growth of Metrobus Ltd from its inception in 1983 to the present day. It explains the steps taken to achieve this growth and outlines many of the company's developments over these ten years. Present day operations are highlighted and details of vehicles owned, past and present, are included. It is my hope that this book will appeal to the more general reader as well as the dedicated bus enthusiast.

I wish to thank those who have helped in the preparation of this publication, especially Peter Larking, Gary Wood and the staff of Metrobus, Joel Kosminsky, Mike Harris, Graham Sanders, and all my colleagues and friends who have put up with my "book talk" over the past year.

Blackheath, September 1993   ANDREW BOAG

Introduction

Metrobus Ltd began operations on 24th September 1983 when the services of Tillingbourne (Metropolitan) Ltd were taken over by two directors of the latter company, Peter Larking and Gary Wood. This followed the collapse, in February 1981, of the Orpington & District bus company, which had previously operated a small network of services linking the Croydon area with Orpington and Biggin Hill, and provided the sole bus service to the Forestdale Estate at Addington. The Orpington & District operation had been in financial difficulties for some time and it was no great surprise that the company folded.

From very humble beginnings, with a handful of second hand vehicles, Metrobus has grown steadily year by year and now boasts a modern fleet of over seventy buses and coaches. The directors of the company were convinced that they could attract custom on new routes in areas poorly served by existing London Transport operations. From the outset Metrobus was determined to provide a high quality service which passengers could depend on. Whilst national bus usage has been falling (a process arguably accelerated outside London by deregulation in 1986), Metrobus has increased usage of its services each year since inception. Indeed, some of its innovations have been so successful that additional capacity has been required and increased frequencies, and/or larger vehicles, have been introduced.

Metrobus Limited is a private limited company, set up and owned by its two directors, Peter Larking and Gary Wood, and is completely independent of other bus operators. It has no financial interest in other companies and exists to provide bus and coach services along with certain related activities. The company has managed to be profitable throughout its existence.

The blue and yellow buses of Metrobus are now a familiar sight in south east London and the company also includes a thriving coaching arm. From the outset dual-purpose coaches were operated on a limited excursion programme. Metrobus inherited these operations from the Tillingbourne Bus Company, including a popular coastal service from Orpington to Brighton. A number of coach companies in the Bromley area have been acquired, most notably Southland Coaches, whose trading name has been continued. More recently, local company Jason's Coaches, has been taken into the fold although in this case its identity has not been perpetuated.

Metrobus today operates nine regular bus services, one express commuter coach service to central London, and three seasonal 'Coastlink' services. It has twenty coaches of various specifications (including one double-decker) for use on contracts, excursions and private hire work. The bus services are provided under Section 3(2) of the London Regional Transport Act, 1984. This provides for LRT to secure services from third parties, whether by tender, contract or commercially, and Metrobus routes fall into all three categories. Services 61, 146 and 261, previously operated by LRT's subsidiary, London Buses Ltd, are tendered to Metrobus, whereas the original services, 353, 354 and 357, are contracted. The 351, 356 and 358 are commercially operated under a London Bus Agreement within the same Act. Route 705 is operated under a London Bus Agreement for the section within the Greater London area and is registered with the Traffic Commissioners for the rest. Coastlink services 350,355 and 365, together with the short-lived 739, operate under a London Local Service licence for the portion of route within Greater London, and are registered commercial services outside London. Metrobus is now a significant employer with staff numbers having grown from six to one hundred and sixty.

In the future, Metrobus looks set to meet challenges brought about by the privatisation of London Buses, the operating subsidiaries of London Transport. The government has planned to extend the concept of free competition to London for some years, but so far appears to be reluctant to take the plunge. In some towns and cities outside London deregulation has led to 'bus wars' with competing operators racing each other to stops on busy routes, whilst unprofitable off-peak services have been reduced. The overall effect has been to undermine public confidence in bus services, and further measures may be necessary to ensure a more satisfactory outcome in London. There is little doubt that serious traffic problems could develop if intensive competition arises.

Metrobus feels that the present system of tendering in London has stimulated competition, but it does not offer much incentive for innovation by operators. Bus planning in London has become more centralised in recent years and service changes tend to be based on computer generated interpretations of passenger surveys. By contrast, most of the services introduced by Metrobus have been based on extensive local knowledge. They have been carefully designed to serve new markets and provide additional links to established centres. A complete free-for-all is not considered to be the best way forward, but there needs to be a process by which innovative developments can be encouraged within a regulated framework.

How Metrobus was set up

The Tillingbourne Bus Company is a long-established and respected independent operator, based in Cranleigh, Surrey which played a very important role in the formation of Metrobus. Although in west Surrey, over thirty miles from Orpington, the company saw the potential of operating the former Orpington & District services. Tillingbourne stepped in at very short notice to provide a peak hour service between Forestdale and Croydon, via Coombe Road, from 2nd March 1981. Forestdale is a substantial modern housing development which had never been served by London Transport services. Had Tillingbourne not stepped in, the area - which is over five miles from its nearest railway station, at East Croydon - would have been without public transport.

Tillingbourne set up a separate subsidiary company, Tillingbourne (Metropolitan) Ltd under the control of Gary Wood and Peter Larking, together with a third director, Mark MacWilliam, who subsequently departed to pursue other interests. The new company worked hard to restore public confidence in these services. It was recognised that a new public image coupled with 100% reliability would be needed if the new operation was to succeed. This was especially important given the low frequency of the services compared to others in the London area and the poor reliability of Orpington & District in their latter days.

Apart from the Croydon approaches at peak times the routes operated did not suffer from heavy traffic congestion. The careful recruitment of dedicated staff meant that they were unaccustomed to some of the more dubious practices which plagued London's bus services for so many years. In 1982, 14% of LT's bus mileage was not operated for various reasons, a level rarely matched outside the capital, whilst timekeeping left a lot to be desired. Tillingbourne set out to improve these standards to match those achieved by its other operations. These standards still apply to Metrobus operations today, the company having maintained an enviable record of reliability.

The elderly Orpington & District fleet was in poor condition and none of its buses was considered suitable for the new Tillingbourne operation. Instead, Tillingbourne provided modern single deck vehicles from its Cranleigh base plus two new dual-purpose AEC Reliance coaches (the last AEC vehicles built) from a cancelled Green Line order.

By late 1981, the full potential of the Orpington based operations had become clear and at this time three basic services were operated:-

353   Croydon - Coombe Road - Coney Hall - Locks Bottom - Orpington
      (Monday to Friday peak hours)
355   Croydon - Coombe Road - Forestdale
      (Monday to Friday peak hours)
357   Croydon - Coombe Road - Forestdale - Coney Hall - Locks
      Bottom - Orpington (Monday to Saturday, all day)

The 357 provided a basic hourly service, supplemented by the 353 and 355 at peak times, giving a maximum of three buses per hour into Croydon.

On 4th May 1982, Bromley was served for the first time by Tillingbourne (Metropolitan) buses. New 'shoppers' route 354 was introduced, running from Sanderstead to Bromley (Churchill Theatre) via Selsdon, Forestdale and New Addington. Just one off-peak return journey was provided on Mondays to Fridays. This is in stark contrast with today's operations where Metrobus operates over forty buses per hour through Bromley town centre at peak times.

After eighteen months Peter Larking and Gary Wood made an offer to buy out the Cranleigh based shareholders of the Tillingbourne (Metropolitan) operation. Patronage of the Orpington-based operations was steadily increasing and they were becoming more lucrative than those in Tillingbourne's home territory in Surrey. Suitable terms were agreed with the parent company enabling the two operators to go their separate ways. The transfer took effect from Saturday 24th September 1983.

Metrobus acquired the former Tillingbourne (and Orpington & District) premises at Oak Farm, Green Street Green as an operating base, along with six staff and the same number of vehicles. These comprised two dual-purpose AEC Reliance coaches with Duple bodies (one of which remains in stock today), one AEC Reliance bus with a Duple bus body, two Bedford YMTs (one having Plaxton dual-purpose bodywork and one bus style by Duple), and one Bristol VRT double decker.

METROBUS LIMITED

take over Tillingbourne Metropolitan services from 24 September 1983.

Cheque payments for season tickets coach hire and excursions should be made out to Metrobus Ltd. from this date.

- Same reliable service
  - Same management & staff
    - New fleetname...

METROBUS

The Bus Garage, Oak Farm,
Farnborough Hill, Orpington,
Kent BR6 6DA

Telephone:
Farnborough 61432

1983 - The Early Days

On that first September morning most passengers boarding their usual bus would have been oblivious to the change in ownership. In 1983 the London bus scene was nothing like as colourful as it is today, standard red buses dominating most areas. Green buses and the Green Line coaches of London Country Bus Services (part of the National Bus Company) were familiar, but very few other operators were licensed to operate within the Greater London area. The livery chosen for the new company was blue and yellow, very similar to but slightly brighter than that of the Tillingbourne company which had been so inspirational in the formation of Metrobus.

How it all began. Duple bodied AEC Reliance JTM 109V stands in the Depot at Green Street Green on the morning of Saturday 24th September 1983. It performed the first ever Metrobus service on route 357 from Orpington to Croydon. The Tillingbourne blue, yellow and white livery is still carried, but the fleetnames have been painted out. *P Gooderson*

In 1983 London Transport was under the control of the Greater London Council. Its Labour leader, Ken Livingstone, was intent on pursuing a low fares policy for London, subsidised from the rates. Following the short-lived 'Fares Fair' regime in 1981/2, fares on London Transport services had been doubled in March 1982. Further changes had been made to the LT fares structure in May 1983, when Travelcards were introduced, offering for the first time a joint Underground and bus season ticket. However, the cheap fares on London Transport services were not extended to Metrobus passengers, who, nevertheless, were mostly London ratepayers. As such, the company made a case for its passengers to also receive the benefit of cheap travel, and this was the first step towards the harmonisation of Metrobus services within the LT network.

The first service changes implemented by the new company took effect on 24th October 1983. New timetables were introduced, and the 354 was altered to run from Croydon via Forestdale to Coney Hall (omitting New Addington), and then on to Bromley, via Hayes and Bourne Vale. The Bourne Vale routeing had been introduced eleven months earlier, following requests from residents, whose homes were some distance from existing LT services. Prior to that the service had operated via Pickhurst Lane and Westmoreland Road. The frequency remained unchanged at this stage.

The early popularity of the 357 service is very evident in this view of AEC Reliance JTM 109V picking up passengers in Spur Road, Orpington. *John Gaff.*

Left: Peak hour services between Croydon and Orpington which do not serve Forestdale are numbered 353. In this 1983 view of AEC Reliance ODV 404W, Director Peter Larking picks up passengers at Spur Road, Orpington. *Laurie James*

Right: The sole double decker acquired from the Tillingbourne (Metropolitan) fleet, a Bristol VRT, awaits passengers at Fairfield Halls, Croydon. *Maurice Doggett.*

Coastlink service 350 was operated by Metrobus for just one weekend in September 1983 before its seasonal withdrawal for the winter. This rare view from 1983 shows Reliance ODV 405W having returned to the Depot, alongside the sole Plaxton bodied vehicle in the fleet at that time, SPA 192R, a Bedford YMT. *John Gaff*

1984 - A Year of Consolidation

Following the establishment of the new company the previous year, 1984 turned out to be relatively quiet for Metrobus. This gave the company the opportunity to build on its success. Passenger numbers were continuing to increase and political developments began to create an opportunity for further prospects of expansion in future years. The 1984 Transport (London) Act took control of London Transport away from the Greater London Council, which was later abolished. This came into effect on 29th June, when London Regional Transport became accountable directly to the Department of Transport. Two main operating subsidiaries, London Buses Ltd and London Underground Ltd, were established, taking over former LT services in the London area. Both companies received an operating subsidy covering all services including those outside the former Greater London Council area, which had not been the case previously.

The main effect of the Act on Metrobus was that London Regional Transport was required to seek tenders for the operation of bus services. Given that very few bus services in London were able to make an overall profit, the opportunities for cost savings were great and the choice of routes to tender was very extensive. Thirteen routes were chosen for the first round, including route 146 between Bromley North Station and Downe (via Hayes and Keston). This was a lightly-used, single-deck service with an approximately hourly frequency for most of the day and no Sunday service. Metrobus decided to submit a bid to operate the 146.

Bedford single deckers have formed an important part of the Metrobus fleet over the years. This view shows a Duple Dominant bodied YMT laying over in Mortimer Road, Orpington shortly before the stand was taken out of use. *Metrobus*

In 1984 route 354 had just one return journey, provided by a spare off-peak vehicle from the 353/357 allocation. AEC Reliance JTM 109V prepares to leave Forestdale for Bromley. *John Gaff*

During the summer of 1984, certain journeys on route 357 were extended from Orpington to Hewitts Farm. The extension was not well supported and did not operate in future years. The DMS in the background was later acquired by Metrobus for spares. Park Royal bodied AEC Reliance JPA 140K is seen leaving the farm en route for Croydon in July. This vehicle was at that time on loan to Metrobus and was subsequently purchased, having started life as a Green Line coach with London Country. *Graham Sanders*

Summer 1984 saw the extension of the coastal service 350 from Brighton to Worthing, via Shoreham. This attracted good custom in the generally favourable weather experienced that year, and duplicate journeys were operated on some occasions. Another seasonal feature, introduced as an experiment, was the extension of certain journeys on route 357 to Hewitts Farm, at Chelsfield from 12th May. Hewitts Farm is one of the largest 'Pick-your-own' fruit and vegetable farms in the London area; at that time the farm also ran its own network of free bus services during the summer season. Unfortunately the 357 extension was not well supported and it was never repeated after its seasonal withdrawal on 1st September. The Company produced a day excursion brochure for the first time, listing almost thirty days out. These contained many pick-up points in the Orpington area and were concentrated at weekends, when spare vehicles were available.

Meanwhile, on the vehicle front, the Bristol VRT was replaced by two Northern Counties bodied Daimler Fleetlines purchased from West Riding (BHL 609/624K). These arrived in August, and one (609) immediately received an overall painted advertisement for Bristol Street Motors. These acquisitions provided additional capacity at peak times, which was to become much needed the following year.

Two Northern Counties bodied Daimler Fleetlines were purchased from West Riding in August 1984. BHL 609K enters the depot for the first time at the end of its long journey from Yorkshire, followed closely by sister vehicle BHL 624K. *Metrobus*

1985 - Fair Fares and New Opportunities

The year 1985 began with a fares revision on 6th January. Following negotiations with London Regional Transport, terms were agreed for fares on Metrobus services to be reduced to standard LRT levels. GLC/London Borough pensioners' and handicapped persons passes had always been accepted by Metrobus; most other London Regional Transport passes were also included in the new agreement, with LRT making up the revenue shortfall by means of an agreed formula. A new London-wide ticket, the Capitalcard (later merged with the Travelcard) which had been planned by the now defunct GLC for some years, was introduced at this time. This had similar bus and Underground availability to a Travelcard, but included British Rail travel at a small extra charge. These new conditions had a dramatic effect on the usage of Metrobus services. Passengers no longer had to pay a premium on Metrobus routes, and the ability to transfer to BR without a separate ticket was an added bonus.

Within a few months the number of passengers using Metrobus services had increased significantly. The strongest effect was felt between Forestdale and East Croydon, where many former car users had transferred to bus. Metrobus was hard pressed to cope with the demand at peak times and purchased a further AEC Reliance dual-purpose coach from Ravensbourne Coaches to supplement the one already on loan. This was used to duplicate certain peak journeys until 29th July when timetables were revised.

In the spring LRT announced tender results for the first batch of routes. Route 146 was awarded to Crystals Coaches, to take effect from 10th August 1985. Although disappointed by failing to win this tender, the company was soon to be given much greater opportunities to operate LRT routes.

Such were the fortunes of the company in 1985 that it was possible to purchase its first brand new bus. The smart 77-seat Leyland Olympian with Eastern Coach Works bodywork, entered service on 1st August 1985, proudly proclaiming its first day 'C' registration, C395 DML. It was the first ECW bodied Olympian to be sold new to a private operator, and the first new double decker to enter the fleet of an independent London bus company since the 1930s. Although mostly used on the 357, it made frequent trips to the coast during the summer months, on the Coastlink service, and was also available for private hire work.

The first new bus purchased by Metrobus was this ECW bodied Leyland Olympian, C395 DML which entered service on 1st August 1985. It is seen here whilst still brand new at Courtwood Lane, Forestdale.
John Gaff

The other major event of the summer of 1985 was the announcement by LRT of a major reorganisation of services in the Orpington area. A significant feature was that almost all routes serving the town would be put out to tender. A number of local routes would be operated by midibuses with a capacity of 20-25 seats. These proposals presented major opportunities for Metrobus.

The company had by now established its credibility and was ready to expand. Metrobus had drawn up its own plans to provide bus services to poorly-served parts of the Orpington area, utilising buses spare from the 357 in Monday to Friday off-peaks and during layovers. Buses would have continued to Green Street Green via Sevenoaks Road, Repton Road, Eton Road, The Highway, Windsor Drive, Vine Road and Worlds End Lane.

A new hourly route would have been introduced on Mondays to Saturdays between Darrick Wood Estate and St Mary Cray via Starts Hill Road, Farnborough Way, Tubbenden Lane, Station Road, Orpington High Street, Lancing Road, Court Road, Ramsden Estate, Chelsfield Road, St Mary Cray High Street, then a one-way loop via Hearn's Rise, Barnfield Road and Augustine Road, returning via Chalk Pit Way to St Mary Cray High Street. Although favourably received by LRT, from whom agreement to operate a bus service was required, neither proposal came to fruition. LRT was already planning its own network of new bus services in the Orpington area, which was to be introduced in August 1986, with routes serving many of the areas in the Metrobus proposals.

The gradually expanding fleet and the prospects for future expansion dictated a need for improved garage facilities. This was achieved by acquiring a six-bay workshop from the defunct Continental Pioneer Company of Richmond. It was moved to Green Street Green and re-erected on land adjacent to the original Metrobus garage.

Private hire operations continued to prosper in 1985 and a programme of excursions was organised, which included four-day extended tours to the Lake District and to Wales.

Outwardly very similar to existing AEC Reliances in the fleet, this Bedford YMT with 53-seat Duple bodywork was purchased from Eastern National in March 1985. It is seen here on diversion in Orpington High Street, being driven by Norman Pinnegar, the company's longest serving driver. *Graham Sanders*

This Bedford YMT arrived from Maidstone Borough Council in February 1985. It had 61 seats achieved by a three and two seating arrangement towards the rear of the bus. This September 1985 view at Hayes Station shows passengers boarding on route 354 bound for Bromley. Driver Derek Parker had benefited from a change in the law which reduced the minimum PSV driving age to 18. He still works for Metrobus today, now holding the position of Assistant Chief Engineer. *Graham Sanders*

1986 - Success with LRT

The year began quietly with the company preparing its bids for the Orpington LRT bus network. In April it was announced that Metrobus was to take over the 61 from London Buses. At that time the route ran from Bromley North to Eltham Station via Orpington and Chislehurst; the original intention had been to split it in two at Orpington. In the event the route was cut at Chislehurst, the Eltham section becoming the 61B. However, on Sundays the service would continue to Eltham. The frequency of the new service would be every 12 minutes at peak times, requiring ten buses, and resulting in a significant increase in the fleet size. This represented a major challenge for the company; could it continue to provide the same quality of service on a major route as it had achieved with a small operation?

The company was determined to ensure that its reputation would be enhanced by this award. Metrobus had actually submitted three tenders for the 61. The first involved the use of new Bedford single-deck buses, the second featured new Leyland Olympian double deckers, and the third offered second hand double deckers. In the event LRT chose the third option. At that time London Buses was selling surplus DMS class Fleetline double deckers, allegedly unsuitable for London conditions. Many went to provincial operators who had found that once 'London' modifications such as automatic gearboxes were removed, their reliability was quite acceptable. Accordingly, Metrobus decided to buy thirteen examples from the bus dealer Ensign (KUC 898/922/960P, OUC 52/54/56R, OJD 167/173/198/200/211/243R). All had MCW bodywork and were fitted with one additional seat on the upper deck before entering service giving a total seating capacity of seventy. This was achieved by replacing the single seat behind the staircase with a double seat. The DMSs were the first full-height buses owned by Metrobus; earlier double deckers including the new Olympian had all been 'low height' 13ft 8in versions due to the low railway bridge in Coombe Road, Croydon. However, after this bridge was demolished (the Woodside to Sanderstead line having closed in 1983), it ceased to be a problem. In the event it became rare for DMSs to operate on the Croydon routes until the 356 appeared.

In addition to the thirteen DMSs came three new Bedford YMT single deckers with Wadham Stringer bodies seating 53 passengers plus 18 standees (D21-23 CTR). These would mainly operate on the Croydon routes. A further use for these buses came with the late announcement from London Regional Transport that Metrobus had been awarded an extra service in the Orpington network. Existing London Buses route 261

Three new Bedford YMTs with Wadham Stringer bodywork arrived in August 1986. Intended primarily for the Croydon routes they were also frequently used on route 361. This view taken at East Croydon shows passengers boarding D22 CTR on route 357. Construction of the new law courts can just be seen in the background. *John Gaff*

(Lewisham and Orpington, via Farnborough) had been cut back to Bromley Common under the original proposals, its replacement being new midibus route R1. Following public consultation there was some concern over the loss of a long-established direct link from Farnborough and Green Street Green to Bromley town centre. Although Green Line service 706 continued to provide this facility, it was recognised that the hourly service on this lengthy route required supplementing. Accordingly new route 261A, between Bromley North Station and Green Street Green, was tendered and at first awarded to London Buses. London Buses intended to operate this service from Bromley garage but was unable to negotiate suitable terms with local staff due to the tight schedule, which contravened union agreements. As the August deadline for introducing the new network approached, it became clear that agreement would not be reached and LRT re-awarded the contract to Metrobus, as route 361. Just one bus was required for this service in theory, but in practice traffic congestion in Bromley town centre meant that vehicles were often changed at Green Street Green to aid reliability.

Early morning on 16th August 1986, the first day of Metrobus operation on routes 61 and 361. Fleetlines prepare for the early morning run-out at the Green Street Green depot along with Olympian C395 DML allocated to the 357. *Metrobus*

Church Hill, Orpington is the scene for this view of operations by three different bus companies on 16th August 1986 as Metrobus DMS Fleetline OJD 167R passes an ex Strathclyde PTE Leyland Atlantean on route 51, which had been taken over by London Country (South East) on the same day. The Glasgow Atlanteans proved to be less than satisfactory and were soon replaced by newer vehicles. Also visible is a London Buses Leyland Titan on route 208, which was not altered in the Orpington review. *Lyndon Rowe*

Northern Counties Fleetline BHL 609K stands at the Orpington terminus of routes 353 and 357 carrying an overall advertisement for Dees, the Ford Dealer. This replaced the earlier advertisement for Bristol Street Motors. *P Gooderson*

The Orpington scheme proved to be one of the most successful tendering exercises carried out by LRT. The local midibus services were operated by Roundabout, a subsidiary of London Buses' Selkent division, and represented LRT's first major network use of small buses. The new services were introduced without a hitch and were generally welcomed by the travelling public. Metrobus worked closely with LRT to produce a robust schedule for the 61 which would survive the horrors of Bromley traffic. Apart from the Sunday schedule and minor adjustments to evening running times, the basic 1993 timetable for the 61 had not altered since August 1986.

Routes 61 and 357 follow the same routeing between Orpington and Locks Bottom where DMS Fleetline OUC 52R is seen heading for Bromley North whilst Northern Counties Fleetline BHL 624K continues to Forestdale and Croydon.
Graham Sanders

Among the DMSs bought by Metrobus for route 61, three including DMS 1960 were fitted with Leyland engines. The general preference for the Gardner engine fitted to the rest is reflected in the fact that the three Leyland ones were the first to be withdrawn by the company. *G. R. Mills*

In order to improve the control of services, all buses were fitted with two-way radios for route control and emergency purposes. The Company was allocated its own UHF radio channel, and an aerial on high ground at New Addington is connected to base control at Green Street Green via a land line.

Route 354 received a much improved timetable with the August changes following discussions with LRT. The route was revised to operate between Bromley North Station and Selsdon, Farley Road. A basically hourly off-peak service was provided on Mondays to Fridays, utilising buses spare from routes 353 and 357. Use of the number 355 for short journey buses on route 357, between Croydon and Forestdale, was dropped at the same time. The section of route 354 between Selsdon and Croydon was abandoned, although it would later be reinstated, via a new

Northern Counties Fleetline BHL 624K rests in the depot. These vehicles were normally allocated to the busiest duties on route 357, where their high seating capacity was much needed. *G. R. Mills.*

routeing. It had been intended that the 354 would operate via Selsdon Vale in order to serve new housing developments. This was frustrated by strong opposition to the service from some local residents who did not like the idea of buses passing, or stopping, outside their homes. The roads concerned were clearly not ideal for bus operation but many homes were a considerable distance from the nearest bus service, and even in a relatively affluent area not everyone had access to a car. Both Metrobus and LRT were keen to provide a public transport service for Selsdon Vale and eventually, over a year later, agreement was reached.

One national event which was to affect Metrobus in future years was the deregulation of all bus services outside London from 26th October. The company closely monitored developments resulting from this, since it was proposed to extend deregulation to London in due course.

Route 361 was originally to have been numbered 261A and operated by London Buses. The contract was re-awarded to Metrobus before its introduction and the service was given a more distinctive identity. *Mike Harris*

Heavy snow fell during the morning of 14th January 1987 causing major disruption to services. DMS Fleetline OJD 173R drops off passengers at Locks Bottom on route 61. *Graham Sanders*

1987 - Another LRT Route Added

After the new Orpington network few further tendering opportunities were expected locally, as LRT turned its attention to other parts of London. It was a surprise, therefore, when LRT announced in April that it was re-tendering a number of services which had been awarded to London Buses. These services, it had been found, were not covering their full costs. One of the routes involved was the 261 between Lewisham and Bromley Common, via Lee Green, Grove Park and Bromley town centre. Metrobus was successful in its bid for this route, to be taken over from November. Once again, three bids were submitted to LRT on the basis of new, or second-hand, double deckers and new Leyland Lynx single deckers. LRT again opted for the second-hand double deck option.

Olympian C395 DML demonstrates the extremely heavy loads carried on route 357 at peak times as it leaves East Croydon in June 1987. *Colin Fradd*

Mindful of the need to reduce the average age of its fleet to avoid a concentration of vehicles of similar age, the company decided not to purchase further DMSs for this service but to obtain newer vehicles. A side effect of deregulation was that some provincial operators were disposing of modern buses. One such operator was West Yorkshire PTE which offered a number of single door Roe-bodied Leyland Olympians dating from 1982/3. These eleven buses (UWW 13/14/16X, CUB 60/61/63/64/66/68/69/71Y) were purchased by Metrobus via the dealer, Ensign, in July, before the result of the tenders for the 261 was known. Had the company been unsuccessful the Olympians would have been used to upgrade the 61. Somewhat ironically, West Yorkshire PTE used the name 'MetroBus' for services operated on its behalf by operators serving the Metropolitan County, and for some years after their change of ownership the buses retained interior transfers warning passengers against vandalism to 'MetroBus' vehicles. Twenty-five additional drivers were recruited to operate the service.

Two further Leyland Olympians had been purchased in June 1987, XWY 475/476X. These were lowheight ECW bodied examples dating from 1982 and almost identical to C395 DML, purchased new in 1985. Like the Roe-bodied ones they originated from Yorkshire, but this time from the former National Bus Company subsidiary of West Riding (which also provided services for the West Yorkshire 'MetroBus' network). They replaced the Northern Counties Fleetlines on routes 353/357, which were withdrawn and sold.

Metrobus frequently provides vehicles for rail replacement services. This September 1987 view shows two Bedfords, D21 CTR and WKE 67S, outside Penge East station. The first has Wadham Stringer bodywork, the other Duple. *John Gaff*

The growth in fleet size enabled Metrobus to provide replacement bus services for British Rail on a number of occasions. One such example, during October 1987, utilised a number of the then new Roe Olympians between Orpington and Sevenoaks, prior to their use on the 261.

A new timetable was introduced on route 361 from 1st September. The basic service was unaltered but one early morning return journey was extended from Green Street Green to Pratts Bottom, on Mondays to Fridays, to supplement the Kentish Bus 402 service. This took the route into some of the more rural surroundings still within Bromley Borough.

A date which stands out in most people's memories is 16th October 1987, the night of the hurricane. South east London and Kent were particularly affected and Metrobus services were badly disrupted. Nevertheless, Metrobus managed to run a restricted service on all routes before the Police ordered all high sided vehicles off the road, fearing that the high winds would return. Metrobus services that day included a scheduled early morning rail replacement service for Network SouthEast. This was probably the closest thing to a scheduled rail service in south east London on 16th October. For a brief period afterwards Orpington became the end of the line for trains from London to Hastings, Ashford, and Folkestone (via Tonbridge) due to storm damage. Ironically, engineering work had been pre-planned to close the line between Orpington and Sevenoaks the following weekend with buses laid on. Passengers travelling to points beyond Tonbridge were forced to make their own arrangements.

On 31st October 1987, the re-routeing of route 354 via Selsdon Vale was eventually introduced. Agreement had been reached with the London Borough of Croydon, on condition that only single-deck buses would be used on the service. Hail and ride operation was adopted in Selsdon Vale allowing passengers to board and alight at any safe point on the line of route. This arrangement helped to minimise disputes regarding the location of bus stops outside people's houses. However, some residents took exception to timetable frames being installed on lamp posts as this seemed to encourage such points to be treated as recognised stopping places. To coincide with these changes and to provide new links, route 354 was re-extended to Croydon, terminating at Fairfield Halls during shopping hours and East Croydon Station at peak times. From the Farley Road terminus buses ran via Croham Road to Park Hill Road, then via 357 to East Croydon and Fairfield Halls. Single-deck Bedfords became the normal allocation. A revised timetable was introduced on routes 353 and 357 at the same time.

Metrobus took over the 261 on Saturday 21st November. A particular feature of this service is the higher frequency on Saturdays – every 7-8 minutes compared with every 12 minutes on Mondays to Fridays. As a result there were insufficient Olympians available and a substantial part of the Saturday allocation had to be covered with DMSs, a situation which has continued to a lesser extent to the present day. One minor route change took place with the southern terminal becoming Bromley Common, 'The Crown', instead of Bromley Common bus garage (owned by London Buses). The previous terminal had been used by London Buses for operational convenience but this section was not part of the contract and Metrobus did not need to serve it.

Route 261 was taken over by Metrobus on 21st November 1987. CUB 69Y is one of eleven Roe bodied Leyland Olympians purchased from West Yorkshire PTE for the service. The location is Lewisham Bus station which has subsequently been relocated as part of the town centre redevelopment scheme. *Graham Sanders*

An unusual vehicle which spent six months in the fleet during the summer/autumn of 1987 was this Berkhof re-bodied Leyland Leopard, Q856 MEV, which was leased from Southend Transport. It is seen here in Station Road, Orpington. *Graham Sanders*

The only single decker in the fleet to carry an all-over advertisement was Bedford YMT bus AKK 171T. It is seen at Locks Bottom on route 361 in July 1987 and had been purchased from Maidstone Borough Council the previous year. *Graham Sanders*

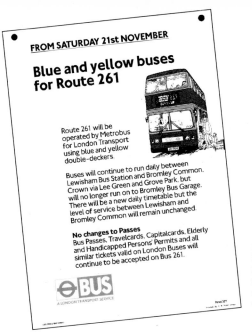

FROM SATURDAY 21st NOVEMBER

Blue and yellow buses for Route 261

Route 261 will be operated by Metrobus for London Transport using blue and yellow double-deckers.

Buses will continue to run daily between Lewisham Bus Station and Bromley Common. Crown via Lee Green and Grove Park, but will no longer run on to Bromley Bus Garage. There will be a new daily timetable but the level of service between Lewisham and Bromley Common will remain unchanged.

No changes to Passes
Bus Passes, Travelcards, Capitalcards, Elderly and Handicapped Persons' Permits and all similar tickets valid on London Buses will continue to be accepted on Bus 261.

⊖BUS
A LONDON TRANSPORT SERVICE

LRT bus stop panel for the introduction of Metrobus to route 261. This style was used for tendered routes generally, with a coloured drawing showing the new operator's livery.

Unlike the 61/361 takeover which had been well-documented in the local press and LRT publicity, there had been very little advance information to passengers about the transfer of the 261 to Metrobus. Many were taken by surprise when a blue and yellow bus turned up at their stop in place of the familiar red one. A timetable leaflet was prepared by LRT and was made available inside buses, as had become standard practice.

Now that Metrobus operations were extending towards inner London it was decided that route 261 buses needed equipment to meet the rigours of urban operation. The buses were fitted with protective screens for drivers and solid plastic seats at the rear of the upper deck, to minimise damage from vandalism.

At the end of 1987 the allocation of vehicles was as follows. Metrobus now had eighty staff to operate and maintain the buses for these services.

	Mon-Fri	Saturday	Sunday
61	10 x DMS	10 x DMS	4 x DMS
261	9 x ONR	14 x ONR/DMS	3 x ONR
353/4/7	3 x ON, 2 x SD	2 x ON	
361	1	1	
TOTAL	25	26	7

Notes

ONR	Leyland Olympian with Roe bodywork
ON	Leyland Olympian with ECW lowheight bodywork
DMS	Ex London Buses Fleetline
SD	Single decker

Route 361 operated with any available vehicle

1988 - Expansion Outside London

The year's most important development, crucial to the company's future success and security, was the purchase of the freehold garage site at Green Street Green. The nation's economy was booming, and industrial land was hard to find, but the site's owners were anxious to liquidate their asset and Metrobus was keen to buy. In May, the freehold of the 2.5 acre site was purchased and developed into a well equipped, low-cost bus operating facility. This work, which took twelve months to complete, included a properly surfaced open bus parking area, new office accommodation, and a staff car park. Certain parts of the site were sold off, most notably to Jason's Coaches. Further details of the Green Street Green garage will be found on pages 84-87

On the bus service front a number of innovative developments, outside the company's normal operating area, were introduced. The first of these was on 1st May, when a new summer only 'Leisureline' service numbered 355 began, with one return journey every Sunday from May to September, and on Wednesdays during August. The service linked Lewisham and Bromley areas with Hastings (first and fifth Sunday in each month and August Wednesdays), the Bluebell Railway and Eastbourne (second and fourth Sundays), or Thorpe Park and Chessington World of Adventures (third Sunday). Seasonal service 350 also resumed from the same date.

Leisureline service 355 began in May 1988 operating each Sunday until the end of September, and on Wednesdays during August. A variety of popular destinations were served, including Thorpe Park as this view of Olympian C395 DML at Bromley Common shows.
Graham Sanders

AEC Reliance ODV 405W passes Bromley South station on the first journey of Metrobus route 705 on 1st June 1988. *Graham Sanders*

The second innovation was the takeover of the commuter coach service between Biggin Hill and Victoria via Bromley, Lewisham and London Bridge. This was previously operated by Interland Coaches. Two return journeys were provided using existing AEC Reliance coaches together with a new DAF coach with 57-seat Duple 320 bodywork, E957 GGX. The route commenced on 1st June as service 705, a number with which Biggin Hill passengers would be familiar, (the former Green Line route 705 having served the area for many years), although the routeing between Lewisham and Victoria was different to that of its Green Line predecessor. Local fares were charged south of Lewisham, but LT passes were not accepted on any part of the route. This arrangement was later changed and they became valid for travel between Bromley and Rotherhithe, following changes to London Buses' route 1.

Since deregulation in October 1986, Metrobus has kept a keen eye on developments outside London. The break up of the National Bus Company and splitting up of the former London Country Bus Services prior to its privatisation had a peripheral impact on services in south east London. London Country South East was privatised in 1988; it was acquired by Proudmutual, a bus holding company based in the North East where it wholly owns Northumbria Motor Services. Shortly before privatisation, London Country South East had changed its name to 'Kentish Bus & Coach' which was more attractive and reflected its main operating area at that time. Gravesend lies at the heart of Kentish Bus operations. It is generally regarded as good bus operating territory, with densely populated areas around the town centre, and large sprawling housing estates containing few local amenities and poor access to rail services.

Metrobus expanded its operating area to include Gravesend on 20th August 1988, when two 'MiniMetro' services began. Reeve Burgess bodied Mercedes F124 TRU heads for Valley Drive on route A with the Thames in the background. *Graham Sanders*

Olympian CUB 60Y received an overall advertisement for Sundridge Park Motors. It is about to depart from Bromley Common terminus for Lewisham with a further Olympian behind. *P Gooderson*

After a detailed study of the area, Metrobus decided that Gravesend and its peripheral housing estates offered considerable potential for additional services. Accordingly, notice was given of its intention to operate a network of 25-seat minibuses in Gravesend. Until that time Metrobus had been reluctant to join the minibus bandwagon, principally because it believed in paying staff a standard rate and staff costs are a major factor in the operation of bus services. It had felt that minibuses provided few advantages over larger vehicles with their greater passenger capacity. Eight minibuses were leased for this experiment which meant that they could be returned if the routes were unsuccessful (or too successful!). They were Mercedes 709Ds, with Reebur bodies (F121-128 TRU). The routes chosen generally paralleled existing Kentish Bus services, but opened up new cross-town links. The initial network, which began on Saturday 20th August comprised:

Route A   Northfleet, (Plough) to Hever Court Road, via Town Centre, Denton and Valley Drive.

Route B   Painters Ash to Hever Court Road, via Town Centre, Denton and Valley Drive.

Both services operated every 20 minutes on Monday to Saturday, combining to provide a 10-minute service on the common section between the Town Centre and Valley Drive. Fares ranged from 20p to 90p, with a maximum return fare of £1.30

MiniMetro route B originally ran from Painters Ash to Valley Drive, providing a joint ten minute service with route A over common sections. Mercedes F126 TRU is seen in Gravesend town centre in September 1988. *Graham Sanders*

The new services were marketed under the name 'MiniMetro', which was displayed on the outside of the vehicles and in all publicity material. Despite the distances involved, all buses were based at the existing Green Street Green garage. To have opened a new local operating base would have considerably increased the cost of the operation, which was in any case an experiment. The company had already gained valuable experience in operating services away from its local area, in early Tillingbourne days. To assist operation and reduce costs, vehicles did not return to Green Street Green for crew changes, during the day, since drivers stayed with their vehicles throughout their shift.

Kentish Bus did not stand back and allow Metrobus to poach passengers. Its first move was to reduce fares on local services from 22nd August, as well as introducing a new discounted multi-journey ticket, to encourage brand loyalty. Although the MiniMetro routes were already well covered by Kentish Bus double deckers, Kentish Bus inaugurated its own minibus network in Gravesend from 17th October, replacing a 30-minute double deck service on their route 12 with a 10-minute minibus service. This followed the MiniMetro routes between Denton and town centre continuing to Northfleet by a different route, and had an introductory fare of 10p. Shortly before this, on 12th October, Black Horse Buses, a company formed by former Kentish Bus employees, started operations in the town using a motley collection of second-hand double deckers in direct competition with all operators along the Gravesend to Denton corridor, including MiniMetro.

A leaflet promoting the new MiniMETRO services in Gravesend

The first of seven Leyland Lynxes in the current Metrobus fleet arrived in September 1988. Brand new F80 SMC approaches Orpington on route 357 in the slightly lighter shade of blue in which it was delivered and before the application of fleetnames. It quickly received standard livery.
Graham Sanders

A further new bus arrived in September, in the form of a Leyland Lynx single decker, F80 SMC. This model replaced the Leyland National, which had become so common throughout Britain during the 1970s, though never operated by Metrobus. Olympian UWW 16X was withdrawn following the new arrival. The Lynx was mostly used on route 361 where its improved acceleration assisted timekeeping, but it also found its way on to other routes, especially the 354.

In Bromley, work on the town centre relief road was progressing and as part of the first stage, Bromley High Street was closed to all vehicles, except southbound buses, between Market Square and Elmfield Road from 6th November. Northbound buses were also diverted from West Street, reaching Bromley North via London Road and Tweedy Road. With cars compelled to use the new Kentish Way and Elmfield Road, instead of the High Street, conditions for buses improved slightly, but these improvements were short-lived, as buses were relegated to part of the new relief road in subsequent phases. Furthermore, road construction work around Bromley North station exacerbated the already appalling local traffic conditions in the short term. Delays of fifteen minutes were commonplace, and had an inevitable impact on the regularity of all bus services. As the delays were reasonably predictable, steps could be taken to minimise their effects. Metrobus was forced to introduce an almost permanent route control point at Bromley North for much of the day.

Various fine tuning measures were made to the Gravesend MiniMetro network. On 14th November, Route A was extended from Northfleet to Swanscombe, and route B was diverted at Painters Ash, to serve Coldharbour. Cheap day return fares became available at all times on Mondays to Fridays, instead of after 0900 only. Hail and ride operation was introduced, with buses stopping anywhere it was safe to do so between Hever Court Road and Mackenzie Way, and throughout the Painters Ash and Coldharbour area. A few weeks later, on 4th December, Sunday services were introduced on route A, between Gravesend and Swanscombe, and on route B, between Gravesend and Painters Ash.

1989 - A Year of Big Changes

This was a year of extensive route changes to the Metrobus network. The first of these were in Gravesend, where routes A and B were revised from 8th April, and a new Sunday route C added:-

Route A   Singlewell to Swanscombe Village, via Valley Drive, Denton, Gravesend town centre and Northfleet. (Monday to Saturday)

Route B   Kings Farm to Painters Ash via Valley Drive, Denton, and Gravesend town centre. (Monday to Saturday)

Route C   Kings Farm Estate via Route B to Town Centre then Colyer Road, Mitchell, Waterdales, Springhead Road, Northfleet, and as route A to Swanscombe. (Sunday only)

Services A and B continued to run every 20 minutes whilst route C provided an hourly Sunday service. MiniMetro was still facing competition from Kentish Bus and Black Horse Buses (later replaced by Autoreps). Some of the rival operations were erratic, but MiniMetro concentrated on providing a reliable service and usage remained healthy. Metrobus had undertaken an extensive marketing campaign to promote MiniMetro, including door-to-door timetable leafleting. It was estimated that some two-thirds of MiniMetro passengers had not previously been regular bus users.

Route 358 began on 13th May 1989, starting with just two off-peak journeys on Mondays to Fridays only, a far cry from the regular 20-minute service of today. AEC Reliance ODV 404W is at Green Street Green during the first week of operation. At that time vehicles for the service were provided from the 705 allocation. *Graham Sanders*

GRAVESEND AREA ROUTES 1988

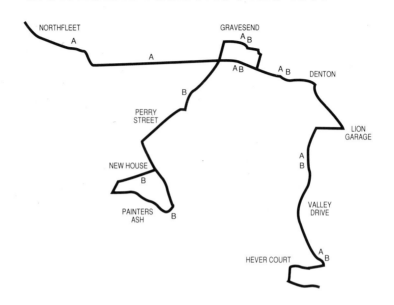

GRAVESEND AREA ROUTES 1989

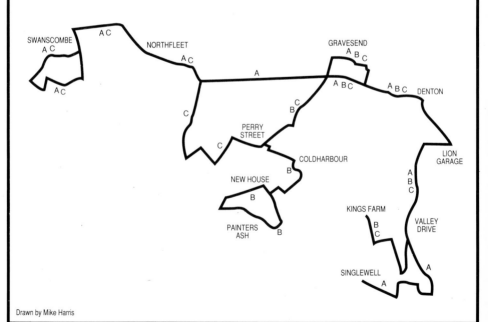

Drawn by Mike Harris

The Gravesend MiniMetro operation by Metrobus came to an end on 31st December 1989, services being taken over by Kentish Bus. Here, a passenger alights from Mercedes F123 TRU shortly before the transfer, with a Kentish Bus Metrorider in the background in the livery of Northumbria Motor Services. *Dave Hunt*

A number of changes were made to LRT services on 13th May 1989, following proposals put forward by Metrobus. On route 261, certain journeys were extended from Bromley Common, (Crown) to Green Street Green via Farnborough, replacing many route 361 journeys. This led to route 361 being withdrawn during peak periods and evenings, on Mondays to Fridays, and completely on Saturdays. The change was partly an economy measure. Buses on route 261 previously ran empty between Green Street Green Garage and Bromley Common. By running most of these journeys in service, via the 361 route, it was possible to provide an improved service south of Bromley Common, although some lightly-used 'against the flow' peak and evening journeys were lost. On Saturdays an hourly service was provided between Lewisham and Green Street Green during shopping hours, with most garage journeys running in service, although some ran empty south of Locks Bottom.

These changes enabled resources to be reallocated. A Monday to Friday peak hour service was introduced on route 354 without additional cost. These journeys were an immediate success, especially at the Croydon end of the route, where standing passengers became a regular feature. Metrobus would have liked to use double deckers on some of the busier journeys, but was restricted by its commitment to single-deck operation through Selsdon Vale. An hourly Saturday daytime service was introduced on the 354 with these changes.

AKK 171T passes through Coney Hall on route 354 after losing its overall advertisement. The bus was sold in 1989. *Graham Sanders*

From 15th May a new commercial service was started. This followed repeated requests for a direct service linking northern points in the Borough of Bromley with hospitals in the south of the Borough. The 358 route was designed to meet as many of these requirements as possible. From Crystal Palace, the buses ran via Penge, Anerley, Elmers End, Beckenham, Park Langley, Bromley South (Bromley Hospital), Locks Bottom (Farnborough Hospital), Orpington Station, and Orpington Hospital to terminate at Green Street Green Garage. In addition to improving access to hospitals, a number of new links were provided across the Borough. Initially, two return journeys were provided on Monday to Friday, utilising buses spare in the middle of the day. Local fares were charged at LT levels, but no passes were accepted initially.

A further innovation for 1989 was route 739, a special coach service between London Victoria and Brands Hatch, via New Cross, Lewisham, Grove Park, Bromley, Orpington and Swanley. It was operated for major events at the racing circuit and the first day of operation was 16th April. One coach was required. Fares varied according to distance, ranging from £5 return from Victoria to £2 return from Swanley. In previous years Green Line service 739 had been provided between Victoria and Brands Hatch, albeit via a different route.

A further Roe bodied Olympian received an overall advert when CUB 71Y appeared in a turquoise livery to promote Barclays Bank. Shortly after this photograph was taken this section of Bromley High Street was pedestrianised during shopping hours, resulting in permanent re-routeing of services via Elmfield Road and Kentish Way. *Graham Sanders*

This view demonstrates the differences between the ECW and Roe bodied Olympians. ECW bodied XWY 475X on route 61 overtakes the Roe example, CUB 69Y, on the 261 at Bromley South. *Graham Sanders*

The seasonal 'Coastlink' services were resumed on Sundays at the beginning of May. Route 355 was revised from its 1988 schedule, losing its Thorpe Park variant, and running to Eastbourne, or Hastings on alternate Sundays. Both the 350 and 355 also ran on Bank Holidays, and on Tuesdays and Thursdays (route 350) and Wednesdays (route 355), during August. Olympian double deckers were normally used on this service.

Details of all these changes were published in a special timetable leaflet, produced by the company, covering all services. This was made available to passengers inside buses along with a further free publication promoting its excursion programme.

Two brand new Leyland Olympians arrived in May. These were the first new double deckers since the arrival of C395 DML in 1985 and formed the first part of a programme to update the fleet by four new double deckers a year. F802/803 NGU were fitted with Leyland bodywork from the Leyland National factory at Workington, the ECW works at Lowestoft having now closed. Although outwardly similar to C395 DML, the new deliveries sounded different due to their Cummins engines instead of the usual Gardner units. Their performance was rather more sprightly too, although fuel consumption was heavier. Internally the buses were to 'DipTac' specification. This meant several modifications to assist passengers, such as colour contrasting grab-rails, illuminated 'Bus Stopping' signs, and forward-ascending staircases. The new buses were immediately put to work on routes 353 and 357 routes (replacing earlier Bedfords WKE 67S and AKK 171T), together with 'Coastlink' services and private hire work.

Leyland Olympian CUB 71Y became an all-over advertisement for Barclays Bank on 5th May, joining two other advert buses in the fleet one for Sundridge Park BMW (CUB 60Y) and the other for Saunders Abbott Motors, Beckenham (OJD 243R). The two Olympians were normally allocated to the 261, whilst the DMS was usually to be found in service on route 61.

The summer of 1989 saw much industrial action affecting public transport in London. Occasional one day strikes began on the London Underground in the spring, creating serious traffic congestion in central London, which adversely affected the 705 operation. This action which centred around pay and working conditions later spread to both British Rail and London Buses operations, resulting in complete chaos throughout the Capital. For example, traffic in Lee High Road was often at a standstill by 0530, even delaying the first 261 journey of the day. Metrobus was not affected by the action and responded by using double deckers (including the new Olympians) on route 705 to help commuters reach central London.

The next stage of the Bromley Town Centre pedestrianisation scheme came into effect on Monday 24th July. From that date Bromley High Street was completely closed to traffic between Market Square and Elmfield Road, from 1000 to 1600, although London Transport, Metrobus and London Buses had fought to retain bus access to the High Street.

Two new Leyland Olympians were delivered in May 1989, replacing the ex Maidstone Bedford single deckers and providing increased capacity on the Croydon routes. F803 NGU passes through Keston in July. *Mike Harris.*

Since it would have been confusing to passengers for buses to follow different routeings at different times of day, it was agreed that buses would operate via Elmfield Road and Kentish Way at all times. Apart from worsening traffic congestion in Kentish Way, exacerbated by construction work on The Glades shopping centre, important stops in the High Street and Market Square were no longer served by Metrobus routes. Many of the replacement stopping facilities were less satisfactory, and it was not until 1993 that some of the new stops were equipped with shelters.

In Gravesend, Sunday-only service C was withdrawn after operation on 12th November because of poor patronage. By this time Black Horse had gone out of business, and plans for new town services by Autoreps had not materialised. However, Kentish Bus had become increasingly concerned about the success of the MiniMetro services, and entered into negotiations with Metrobus to purchase the entire operation. Terms were agreed to take effect from 1st January 1990.

December 1989 saw the purchase of three more Leyland Lynxes, D103/104/110 NDW. These were second-hand examples dating from 1987, which had previously been with Merthyr Tydfil Transport. They were destined to replace the remaining Bedford single deckers and increase fleet standardisation with Leyland vehicles.

The imposition of a weight restriction, caused by a weak bridge in Elmers End Road, necessitated a diversion of route 358, via Beck Lane and Churchfields Road from 5th December.

1990 - New Routes, New Buses, New Passengers

1990 began with the transfer of the Gravesend operations to Kentish Bus on 1st January. All vehicles, and some staff, transferred to Kentish Bus, which continued to operate both routes as before, but adjusted some of its existing services, and many previously competitive journeys were withdrawn. Metrobus leased the existing vehicles to Kentish Bus to maintain the services.

The surplus Bedfords were offered for sale. No buyer emerged, so they were retained as spare vehicles for the time being. It soon became usual practice for two Lynxes to operate on route 261 on Saturdays, normally covering the Green Street Green workings, to assist timekeeping and reduce the DMS requirement on that route. The same route on Saturday also began to see ECW Olympians on a regular basis, which had been displaced from the 357 by newer examples. Two further new Olympians, G804/805 SMV, arrived in late January, to commence the conversion of route 61, a process not completed until early 1992. The new buses were identical to the 1989 deliveries. Apart from seeing new vehicles in January, route 61 lost its Sunday extension from Chislehurst to Eltham after the 13th, and the route was therefore standardised to run between Bromley North Station and Chislehurst daily. The Sunday frequency remained half-hourly, but one fewer bus was required for the service than previously.

Plans were announced for a new commercial service 356 from Biggin Hill to Croydon. This would restore a link lost with the demise of Orpington & District some years earlier. Starting at Biggin Hill Valley the route would be via Stock Hill, Leaves Green, Keston, Baston Road, Hayes Station, Coney Hall, Corkscrew Hill, West Wickham and Shirley. The company had identified a demand for the service to run via West Wickham, rather than the existing Metrobus routes into Croydon. It also catered for school children travelling between Biggin Hill and Coney Hall who previously relied on a contract service provided by Jason's coaches. Agreement was reached with LT for passes and Travelcards to be valid on this service and for normal fares to be charged. An hourly service would operate on Monday to Saturday, with certain peak journeys extended to Dunton Green and one Saturday bus to Sevenoaks via Westerham. The new service commenced on 26th March, with an allocation of two of the surplus Bedford single deckers, although various other types were frequently substituted. At the same time, one return journey on route 705 was extended to and from Dunton Green, via Brasted, Sundridge and Westerham.

New route 356 began in March 1990 linking Croydon with Biggin Hill via West Wickham and Keston. Certain journeys were extended beyond Biggin Hill to Dunton Green or Sevenoaks. The first Sevenoaks journey is pictured passing through Keston with Bedford D22 CTR performing. *Graham Sanders.*

The Sunday extension of route 61 to Eltham was withdrawn in January 1991. Leyland engined KUC 898P is seen at Edgebury, Chislehurst on the last day. *Lyndon Rowe*

In preparation for the new 356, which was to be operated by a mixture of single and double-deck vehicles, including DMSs, all buses received new destination blinds which gave improved information on 'via points' for each route. Demolition of the low bridge in Coombe Road also meant that the company was able to lift its ban on full-height double deckers operating in the Croydon area.

Usage of the experimental 358 had been encouraging and Metrobus decided to promote it to a basically hourly daytime service on Mondays to Fridays, from 26th March. At the same time, London Transport passes and Travelcards became valid. As a result of the bridge restriction at Elmers End, it was decided to reroute the service from Crystal Palace, via Anerley Hill, Penge, Beckenham Road, Croydon Road, Upper Elmers End Road and Links Way, to South Eden Park Road and Hayes Lane. This replaced the temporary routeing via Beck Lane and Churchfields Road. Hail-and-ride operation was adopted in South Eden Park Road. DMSs and Lynxes became regular performers on route 358, and passenger numbers soon grew, as people became used to the new facilities offered.

METROBUS
358
Starting Monday 26 March 1990

CRYSTAL PALACE - ORPINGTON
via Anerley, Penge, Beckenham
Elmers End, Eden Park, Park Langley
Bromley and Farnborough Hospital

NEW REVISED ROUTE

KUC 977P passes through Petts Wood bound for Bromley North. This vehicle is now operated on sightseeing tours by a company in New York. *Graham Sanders*

Further timetable changes took effect from 25th March affecting routes 705 and 739. Route 705 had a single round-trip Sunday (and Bank Holiday) service added between Victoria, Sevenoaks and Chartwell. Route 739, previously restricted to Brands Hatch race days only, became a regular Sunday operation, and was also extended to Chartwell and Ightham Mote. These services were marketed as 'Leisureline' in the company's 'Daybreaks and Summer Services' leaflet. They were not well used and were withdrawn at the end of the summer season (23rd September). One Leyland Lynx was the normal vehicle allocation.

From 23rd April additional late night journeys were provided on route 357. The last departure from Croydon had been at 2133, which was too early for passengers returning home after an evening out. Accordingly, two further departures were added, at 2203 to Forestdale, and 2303 to Orpington. Details of these timetable changes were again included in a free leaflet giving details of all Metrobus services.

Until now, Metrobus had not been involved in operating tendered services outside London. However, in April it began operating a Saturday service on Kent County Council route 404 between Sevenoaks and Ide Hill. These journeys were normally covered by a Bedford working from the 356 allocation. This contract was passed to Kentish Bus after 1st September, when the Saturday extensions to route 356 south of Biggin Hill were withdrawn.

A further new Olympian, G806 TMX, arrived in April, and soon found a home on route 61. In May, it was followed by a further one (807), which was not licensed immediately. The summer seasonal services 350 and 355 were reintroduced on 6th May. Route 350 was withdrawn between Sanderstead and Coulsdon and diverted via Hamsey Green, Whyteleafe and the M25. The 355 was re-routed away from the Bluebell Railway, serving Tunbridge Wells instead. For much of the year, a number of buses and coaches had been used at weekends on a BR rail replacement service between Beckenham Junction and Herne Hill while the line was being upgraded for Channel Tunnel trains.

The three Leyland Lynxes purchased from Merthyl Tydfil soon became regular performers on route 354 where they replaced Bedfords. D103 NDW carries a good load as it leaves Bromley for Croydon. *Graham Sanders*

New Olympians such as G805 SMV began replacing Fleetlines on route 61 from February 1990. *Mike Harris*

On 1st August 1990, Metrobus repeated its 1985 move of placing a new bus in service on the first day of the new registration year. This time the vehicle in question was Leyland Olympian H807 XMY (delivered in May) which took a day trip to the Sussex coast the same day, on route 350, in celebration. It then settled down to more mundane duties on route 61. A rather more interesting new vehicle arrived shortly after this, in the shape of the first production model Leyland Tiger coach, with Plaxton 321 bodywork and 57 seats. Destined mainly for the private hire fleet, the coach was frequently put to work on the 705.

With promising results from the upgrading of the 358 in March, it was decided to further increase the afternoon service to a regular hourly frequency on Monday to Friday from 3rd September. It was previously only two-hourly at certain times.

The only highlight towards the end of the year was the operation of route 208 on Boxing Day. This is a tendered route, normally operated by London Buses (Selkent). Four Olympians provided a half-hourly service between Orpington and Catford in atrocious weather conditions of heavy rain and strong winds, lasting all day.

Metrobus was awarded a one day contract to operate London Buses route 208 on Boxing Day 1990. Four new Olympians provided a half-hourly service between Catford and Orpington. F803 NGU is at Petts Wood station in the rain. *Mike Harris.*

1991 - Minibuses Return and Southland Coaches Acquired

A growing awareness of developments in Docklands resulted in discussions with the London Docklands Development Corporation (LDDC) and Olympia & York, developers of the massive Canary Wharf complex. Existing public transport links to Docklands from south of the Thames were very poor and as a result of these negotiations, proposals were submitted to London Transport for three new commuter routes to be introduced in the spring:-

701	Swanley - Sidcup - Eltham - Kidbrooke - Isle of Dogs
702	Green Street Green - Orpington - St Pauls Cray - Chislehurst - Mottingham - Kidbrooke - Isle of Dogs
703	Orpington - Bromley - Downham - Lewisham - Surrey Quays - Isle of Dogs

The existing 705 service would be re-routed via Surrey Quays. As neither the LDDC nor Olympia & York was able to provide sufficient evidence of demand for the new routes, they were not introduced. The diversion of the 705 was, however, successfully implemented.

Four more new standard Leyland Olympians, H808-811 AGX, arrived in the spring for use on routes 61 and 353/357. The earlier Olympians (F802/803 NGU) were cascaded from the 357 group to the 61, to make way for newer examples. Two more Leyland Lynxes, F165/166 SMT, were acquired from Millers of Foxton, Cambridge, in exchange for two Bedfords (D21/23 CTR), and two DMSs (OUC 54R and OJD 173R).

In February LT announced that Metrobus had been awarded the contract for route 146 from August. The company's blue and yellow would finally be replacing Crystals Coaches, which had covered it since 1985. The award thus brought belated success to Metrobus's first ever route tender, and the company planned to buy new Dennis Darts for the service. This was well-timed, as revised conditions for renewing LT contracts were brought into effect shortly afterwards. These terms meant that a route did not have to be retendered when the contract was due to expire if the existing operator's performance had proved satisfactory. No LT tendered services operated by Metrobus have ever been retendered.

This 73-seat Olympian coach was purchased from Thamesway in May 1991 and remains the only double-deck coach in the fleet. It is seen on the M25 near Dunton Green in August 1991. The front upper deck windows have since been altered to match the standard bus design. *Graham Sanders*

New seasonal service 365 between Crystal Palace and Hastings or Eastbourne began in May 1991. Seen with Director Gary Wood at the wheel, Olympian H811 AGX passes Farnborough Hospital, full of passengers hoping to enjoy a pleasant August day in Eastbourne. *Graham Sanders*

Some of the Mercedes midibuses used in Gravesend returned to Metrobus to launch new route 351 between Bromley North and Penge. F128 TRU leaves Bromley North station on the first morning of the new service in March 1991. The buses carried route diagrams on their sides.
Graham Sanders

Such was the success of the 351 that larger buses soon became necessary. These arrived in August in the shape of seven Dennis Darts with 32-seat Plaxton Pointer bodywork. These vehicles also took over operation of route 146 from 10th August. J706 EMX on route 351 and J702 EMX on the 146 head a convoy of buses from Bromley North. *Graham Sanders*

On Saturday 2nd March a further new commercial service started. Route 351 ran from Bromley North Station via Widmore Road, Market Square (returning via London Road and Tweedy Road), then London Road, Farnaby Road, Ravensbourne, Foxgrove Road, Beckenham, Clock House, Churchfields, Birkbeck, Anerley Station, to terminate at Penge, Crooked Billet. A half-hourly service operated on Monday to Saturday until mid-evening. The 351 reinstated a service to the Birkbeck area following the closure of Elmers End bridge. Four of the Mercedes minibuses used in the Gravesend experiment were used (F123/125/126/128 TRU), having been returned from lease to Kentish Bus.

From 27th April a two-hourly Sunday service was introduced on route 357 on a commercial basis, and various improvements were made to the Monday-Friday timetables. All buses on 353/354/357 were extended to Fairfield Halls (some peak journeys previously terminated at East Croydon) and route 354 was introduced in the evenings between Croydon and Forestdale. These changes required one extra bus at peak times. The improvements also gave Forestdale a regular half-hourly service from Croydon all evening.

Route 357 received a Sunday service from April 1991 and from August the new Dennis Darts were allocated. J704 EMX passes through Keston. *Graham Sanders*

With more passengers using route 358, the service was increased from 27th April to half-hourly between Crystal Palace and Locks Bottom (remaining hourly through to Green Street Green), and an hourly Saturday service was added between Crystal Palace and Locks Bottom. By this time DMSs had become the normal vehicle type for the route, which now required four buses.

The usual summer services were introduced from May, with an additional route. New route 365 operated from Crystal Palace, via Penge, Beckenham, Elmers End, Hayes and Green Street Green, to Hastings, or Eastbourne. The 355 and 365 were timed to meet at Green Street Green so that, in the event of poor weather and low patronage, passengers could be transferred to one vehicle which continued to the coast. On return a bus was scheduled to meet it at Green Street Green and drop people off on each route. The advantage of these 'pay-as-you-enter' express services is that passengers can decide on the day whether to make a trip to the coast, depending on the weather. As a result usage varies, but the Company has contingency plans to operate extra vehicles on fine days. Passengers can reserve a seat by phone if they wish.

A Leyland Olympian double deck coach, B688 BPU, was acquired from Thamesway in May. It seats 73 and carries promotional material for the company between decks. A further development for the 1991 summer season was Metrobus operation of National Express service 682, between Dartford and Ventnor, Isle of Wight.

August proved to be a busy month. Seven new Dennis Darts arrived, representing the company's largest single order so far. They were also the the first Darts in the fleet, although a number of demonstration vehicles had been tested. These were to be used on LT route 146 and would also replace the Mercedes minibuses on route 351. The Darts (J701-707 EMX) have 32 seats plus space for 18 standing passengers, the first vehicle of the batch having high-backed coach seats. Once again Metrobus had new buses in service in August with the latest registration letters. The leased Mercedes minibuses were withdrawn immediately, most being sold over a period to Luton & District, for further service.

Route 146 between Bromley North Station and Downe via Hayes and Keston was taken over by Metrobus on Saturday 10th August. An hourly service, requiring one bus is provided for most of the day, with additional buses at peak times and one morning school journey extended from Biggin Hill. On Saturday the service frequency increases to every 45 minutes during shopping hours, using two buses. This allows more time to recover from traffic delays.

The 351 had been a phenomenal success, the Mercedes midibuses having been inadequate from the start. From 10th August the frequency was increased to a bus every 20 minutes, with an hourly late evening service. At the same time the Mercedes minibuses were replaced by larger Dennis Darts seating 32. The routeing in the Anerley area was also revised, with buses running via Anerley Park (Thicket Road, northbound) instead of Oakfield Road. Four buses were required for the revised service, which was promoted by house-to-house distribution of timetable leaflets. The Dennis Darts also took over late evening duties on 354 and 357.

Two further Leyland Lynxes arrived in February 1991. These were acquired from Miller, of Foxton, Cambridgeshire and replaced the remaining Bedford single deckers. F166 SMT is in Kentish Way, Bromley. It was common for two Lynxes to be allocated to route 261 on Saturdays to cover the Green Street Green workings. *Martin Ruthe*

Routes 351 and 358 run parallel for three short sections of route, an example of which is Beckenham War Memorial where J704 EMX is seen. *Brian Speller*

From 18th August Metrobus provided a Sunday service on route 493 between Orpington and Ramsden Estate. This is an LT tendered route operated by London & Country, and the Metrobus journeys provide an unsubsidised service for Ramsden Estate at times when the 493 does not operate. The same buses also work the 357, so the cost of operating the additional journeys is low. One new Dennis Dart is used for the 357/493 joint operations.

The 356 was not left out of this round of developments. From 31st August it was extended from Biggin Hill Valley to Tatsfield (Ship), via Ricketts Hill Road. Tatsfield had previously been served by Kentish Bus route 23 and Surrey County Council provided financial support for this new link. Leyland Lynxes were the normal allocation following this change, as double deckers were unsuitable for the roads between Biggin Hill and Tatsfield. The frequency remained hourly on Monday to Saturday only. Double deckers began operating certain peak journeys on route 354 from the same date to overcome capacity problems.

Metrobus began Sunday services on route 493 from 17th August 1991, operating at times of the day when the route was uncovered by its normal operator, London & Country. New Dennis Dart J702 EMX leaves Orpington station on the first Metrobus journey.
Graham Sanders

Route 356 was extended to Tatsfield from 31st August 1991. Ex Merthyr Tydfil Lynx D104 NDW prepares to leave for Croydon on the first journey. *Graham Sanders.*

Route 358 received an increased service in April 1991, running half-hourly between Crystal Palace and Locks Bottom on Mondays to Fridays with an hourly service through to Green Street Green. DMSs had become the normal allocation. OJD 167R picks up passengers at Elmers End. *Colin Fradd*

In October 1991 it was the turn of the coaching side of the business to experience expansion. Two local Bromley coach companies, Southland Coaches and RB Coaches, were taken over on 1st October following the retirement of their proprietor. Southland Coaches had been based in two depots at Edison Road and Southlands Road in Bromley, which were acquired for other purposes. Two brand new Leyland Tiger coaches with 53-seat Plaxton 321 bodywork, J201/202 FMX were acquired to update the Southland fleet following the takeover. Ten other coaches moved to the Green Street Green base, but many were soon sold. Those remaining were repainted into Metrobus livery with Southlands fleetnames. It was thought prudent to retain the Southlands name in recognition of the goodwill that the company had gained over its fifty years of operations.

The rest of the year passed quietly, with the commencement of a refurbishment programme for the Roe-bodied Olympians, involving new floors, improved seating, new destination displays and some Dip-Tac features.

This Wadham Stringer 'Portsdown' Dart demonstrator spent a week in the fleet when the company was evaluating various types of bodywork for future orders in April 1991. H908 DTP pulls away from the Fairfield Halls terminus at Croydon while Leyland Lynx D110 NDW awaits its departure time. *Graham Sanders.*

1992 - More Dennis Darts and Route Developments

Two more Olympians, J812/813 GGW, arrived in January, to complete the conversion of route 61 to this type from the following month, thus enabling the relegation of remaining DMSs to lighter duties. These Olympians were to be the first of no fewer than fifteen new buses which would arrive during the year, representing a considerable investment by the company. The first route development of 1992 was the extension of both Biggin Hill journeys on route 705 to Dunton Green from 21st April.

July saw the arrival of three more new Olympians, K814/815/816 HMV. Delivered in all-white, they had been acquired from Volvo Leyland stock, and differed from earlier deliveries in that they were to full height (14ft 2in) specification. These were amongst the last 'all Leyland' Olympians produced and were built with a new-style Volvo front end, which would become standard for future Olympians. Metrobus replaced the front ends with the standard 'Leyland' design before all three entered service sporting their 'K' registrations, on 1st August. A further delivery for August service was a Leyland Lynx MkII, K101 JMV, which arrived on the 8th of that month. The Leyland Lynx had also ceased production with the closure of Leyland's Workington factory and this was one of the last to be built. The opportunity was also taken to replace the front end of Olympian coach B688 BPU to match other Metrobus Olympians. Between 7th and 13th September 1992 Metrobus provided several Olympians for an express service between Victoria and Farnborough (Hampshire) for the Air Show.

During 1991/2, the Roe bodied Olympians underwent refurbishment which included new destination blind displays and improved seating. CUB 66Y is seen at Bromley South nearing the end of its journey from Lewisham.
P Gooderson

Negotiating the hilly terrain of Forestdale Estate is brand new Olympian K814 HMV on its first day in service, 1st August 1992. *Lyndon Rowe*

Certain short working journeys on route 354 are now scheduled for double-deck operation but it is unusual for them to reach Bromley. Olympian H811 AGX turns into Elmfield Road, Bromley, in March 1992. *Graham Sanders*

In addition to the Wadham Stringer 'Portsdown' Dart demonstrator illustrated on page 60, this Reeve Burgess Pointer bodied example was also tested on route 356. *Malcolm King*

A day trip to France and Belgium in April 1992 enabled this shot of Leyland Tiger J201 FMX (with Southlands fleetnames) with a local bus in Ypres. *Graham Sanders*

Seen in the pretty village of Finchingfield whilst operating an excursion to Suffolk villages on 25th May 1992 is ex Southlands DAF, ANA 433Y. *Graham Sanders*

In recent years, Metrobus has operated National Express route 682 to the Isle of Wight. Duple bodied DAF coach E957 GGX negotiates the one-way system at Catford in July 1992 with a London Buses Leyland Titan behind.
Graham Sanders

Route 361 was withdrawn completely in November 1992. During its life the route experienced a wide variety of vehicle types. Ex West Riding Olympian XWY 475X, which entered the Metrobus fleet in 1987, is seen here in Farnborough Village, during the last few months of the 361. *Graham Sanders*

A package of route developments was proposed by Metrobus to coincide with revisions to LT tendered services in the Orpington area from 31st October. The main change affected route 358 which would be revised to operate from Orpington Station via Green Street Green, then existing 361 to Bromley, Widmore Road, Market Square, London Road, Beckenham Lane and Shortlands Road to the present line of route. The frequency would be increased to every 20 minutes throughout the route, with an hourly Sunday service. Operation would be with nine new Dennis Darts. A further 20 staff were recruited for the revised service. As a result of these changes route 361 would be withdrawn completely and the Saturday 261 journeys to Green Street Green would also disappear (except for garage journeys). Following discussions with London Transport, it was agreed that peak hour only route 471, operated by Kentish Bus, would also be withdrawn between Orpington Station and Green Street Green.

The almost annual round of improvements to the 353/354/357 took place on the same date. Peak services on the 354 were increased to a basic half-hourly frequency throughout the route, with a 20 minute service between Forestdale and Croydon at certain times. Changes to the 353/357 were more minor, incorporating a few additional journeys, during Monday to Friday off-peak periods. London Transport produced leaflets for these changes, which required one additional single decker.

Delivery of the new Darts for route 358 was delayed and the services did not commence until 21st November, exactly five years to the day since Metrobus took over the 261. The new Darts (K708-716 KGU) differed slightly from the earlier batch, in being the longer 9-metre version with 35 seats. It became usual practice for these Darts not to be mixed with the shorter versions on routes 146 and 351.

The regular Saturday service to Green Street Green on route 261 was replaced by an improved 358 in November 1992. Before the change, Olympian J813 GGW unloads at Locks Bottom, having made a rare appearance on the 261. In common with most double deckers in the fleet it carries a side advertisement for Excel. *Graham Sanders*

Following the 21st November changes the allocation of vehicles to routes on local bus services was as follows:-

	Mon-Fri	**Saturday**	**Sunday**
61	10 x ON	10 x ON	3 x ON
146	2 x DT*	2 x DT	
261	9 x ONR	14 x ONR/ON/DMS	3 x ONR
351	4 x DT*	4 x DT	
353/354/			
356/357	5 x ON, 6 x LX	2 x ON, 4 x LX	1 x DT
358	8 x DT	8 x DT	2 x DT
493	-	-	**
TOTALS	44	44	9

Notes

*	One schoolday journey on route 146 is provided from the 351 allocation.
**	Route 493 Sunday allocation shared with route 357
ON	Leyland Olympian with Leyland or ECW bodywork
ONR	Leyland Olympian with Roe bodywork
DMS	Ex London Buses Fleetline
LX	Leyland Lynx
DT	Dennis Dart. Routes 146/351 use 8.5-metre 32 seaters, route 358 uses 9-metre 35 seaters. Also used on routes 354/357 evening services and 493 Sundays.

An unusual visitor to route 261 for one day in May 1992 was an Iveco Turbo City 100 double decker, J227 DKX. Alongside it is a more conventional 261 in the form of Leyland Olympian CUB 69Y. *Graham Sanders*

Metrobus decided to operate a Boxing Day service on route 358 for the first time in 1992, and diverted it via the grounds of Orpington Hospital. This was the first time the Company operated a 'commercial' service on Boxing Day, but the route was an obvious choice in view of the many hospitals it linked. As a result of this initiative, London Transport reviewed its own plans and awarded Metrobus a one-day contract for route 211. This was a half-hourly, single-deck service, operated with Dennis Darts between Bromley and Sidcup (Queen Mary Hospital) via route 208 from Bromley to Orpington and then Roundabout route R1.

Route 211 ran for just one day, 26th December 1992, between Bromley North Station and Sidcup via Petts Wood and Orpington, covering sections of routes normally used by other services. Dart K708 KGU picks up passengers at Bromley South Station. The route number 211 has since been allocated to a new London General service which uses identical vehicles (albeit in red livery). *Graham Sanders*

1993 - The Tenth Anniversary Year

Towards the end of 1992, further inroads had been made into the remaining DMS fleet and only three, OJD 198/200/243R, were to see service in 1993. Their appearances remained regular on route 261 on Saturdays, but at other times they were held in reserve to cover breakdowns and other emergencies. Another DMS, OJD 200R, was sold in February, but the condition and reliability of the other two remained good, and they were retained. London Buses had withdrawn its last DMSs from regular service during 1992. With the exception of London Buslines in west London (and some open top sightseeing tour buses), Metrobus was the only London operator still using DMSs on regular services, on which over 2,000 had once been scheduled. Vehicles of similar vintage are still common outside London, however, where many bus companies have found it difficult to finance new bus purchases following deregulation.

February 1st saw the takeover of another coaching business when Jason's Coaches became part of the growing Metrobus operation. Jason's depot was adjacent to the Metrobus premises, the freehold having been sold to them by Metrobus in 1988. The acquisition of the business provided a much needed opportunity to expand the garage facilities. Only four of the former Jason's fleet were included in the deal, these being Dennis Javelin coaches dating from 1990 and sporting 'Hoverspeed' livery for the London (Victoria) to Dover service.

The acquisition of Jason's Coaches led to Metrobus operating the Hoverspeed City Sprint service between Victoria and Dover. Hoverspeed services regularly require more than one coach on each departure. Here, service coach K204 GMX, a new Dennis Javelin, is assisted by DAF relief E597 LVH with a further coach behind. *Graham Sanders*

Awaiting their time to enter the bay at Victoria Coach Station on 20th August 1993 are Javelins G428 and G429 YAY. Both vehicles were acquired with the Jason's Coaches business and are primarily allocated to Hoverspeed duties. *Graham Sanders*

From May, the acquired vehicles were supplemented by K203-206 GMX, four new Plaxton Premier bodied Javelins (all in 'Hoverspeed' livery), a similar number of Volvo B10M coaches having been hired pending the arrival of the new vehicles. The Hoverspeed service continues to be operated by Metrobus. One of the new Javelin coaches attended the Brighton Coach Rally in April, prior to being delivered to Metrobus.

In its tenth anniversary year, the company had an annual turnover of £5 million. In the spring, Metrobus submitted bids to operate a number of LT routes in the Bromley area, but in August it was announced that all had been awarded to other operators. This was a disappointment, but not a major setback, since the company maintained a policy of only bidding for selected routes. It has always placed greater emphasis on providing a high quality service than the cheapest service. There is little doubt that further LT contracts could have been won if the company had been prepared to compromise these principles. But that would be like asking Marks & Spencer to become a discount warehouse.

Metrobus knows that it can be profitable without sacrificing its values, and the Gravesend experiment showed that new passengers can be attracted to buses in a deregulated environment. Most Metrobus services are very well patronised, and very few routes have been abandoned. The original Croydon routes are a good barometer of the company's position. In almost every year since 1983, additional journeys have been added, but none have been withdrawn. Indeed many have been provided out of necessity as usage increased to fill buses to capacity. The credit for this must go to the dedication of all the staff, who have worked so hard to maintain the network of safe and reliable bus and coach services.

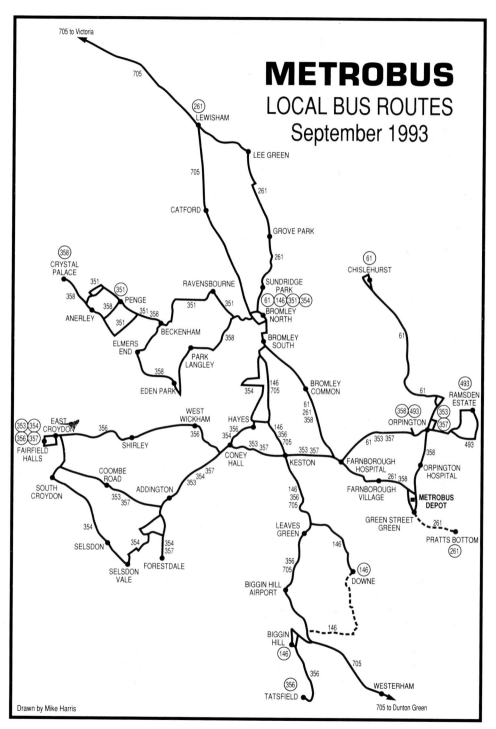

METROBUS
LOCAL BUS ROUTES
September 1993

Drawn by Mike Harris

69

Changes to the 358 enabled the route to serve central Bromley more effectively. Dart K708 KGU passes the 'Greyhound' at Bromley en route for Orpington. *Mike Harris*

Four new Dennis Javelin coaches with Plaxton Premier bodywork arrived in May. Intended mostly for the Hoverspeed service, they also work the 705 between Victoria and Dunton Green. K203 GMX pulls away from the coach stop near Embankment Underground station in July 1993. *Derek Jones*

Leyland Lynx K101 JMV, new in 1992, prepares for service on route 354. *M Johnson*

A sunny Sunday in June 1993 sees new Olympian K815 HMV on route 355 being overtaken by a 1989 example on route 61 at Bromley Common. *Graham Sanders*

A Day in the Life of Metrobus

This chapter aims to tell the story of one day in the life of Metrobus in 1993, and is the result of observations and discussions with some of the staff who organised operations at the Green Street Green base that day.

The date is Wednesday 7th July 1993. The world's most powerful leaders are in Tokyo for the start of the 'G7' Summit. England's cricketers are recovering from the Trent Bridge Test Match against Australia, which they had almost won the previous day. The BBC shows the penultimate episode of Eldorado and the government announces that Oxleas Wood is to be saved from having a motorway through it. For Metrobus it is just another day.

Running a bus and coach company is a twenty-four hour a day operation. The last bus of the previous day returns to the depot just before 0100 hours, and the first departure is at 0500, so there are just four hours when the entire bus fleet is garaged. The coach fleet is less predictable and there are few occasions when every vehicle is off the road. The Hoverspeed contract, between London Victoria and Dover, operates throughout the night, and drivers regularly stay with their coaches at the Dover terminal. Careful scheduling ensures that coaches are refuelled, washed and cleaned at Green Street Green daily, although drivers often change over at the Black Prince interchange, on the A2 in Bexley.

Night Foremen Dave Todd and Robin Smith have prepared the fleet for the early morning run out, and allocated a specific 'running number' to each bus, which is carried on the side of the vehicle. During the course of the day most buses will see several different drivers, for example, running number 1 will be driven by drivers allocated to duty nos. 1,19, 28 & 26. At 0445 the first driver, John Redgate signs on, checked in by Bob Lancaster, one of two Controllers covering the early shift. The next task for drivers is to log in to the Wayfarer ticket and revenue control system, and to collect the appropriate duty card, giving full details of their shift. The driver then goes outside into the depot area to find the bus allocated to his duty and prepares to depart. This is not difficult since Dave Todd has parked vehicles in order of their departure time. Most vehicles are also stored according to their type (such as Dennis Darts, Leyland Lynxes, Olympians and coaches) and the aim is to minimise movements in the depot. Prior to departure, the driver checks the vehicle's water level, inserts his module into the Wayfarer ticket machine, and sets the destination blinds.

The first bus, Olympian CUB 68Y carrying running no.1, leaves the depot on time at 0500. It is initially scheduled to run out of service as far as Farnborough Hospital at Locks Bottom. At 0505 duty no.1 begins its

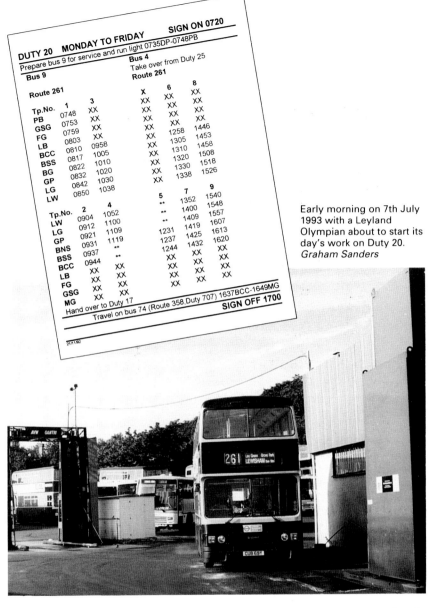

SIGN ON 0720

DUTY 20   MONDAY TO FRIDAY

Prepare bus 9 for service and run light 0735DP-0748PB

Bus 9 — Route 261

Bus 4 — Take over from Duty 25 — Route 261

Tp.No.	1	3	X	6	8
PB	0748	XX	XX	XX	XX
GSG	0753	XX	XX	XX	XX
FG	0759	XX	XX	XX	XX
LB	0803	XX	XX	XX	XX
BCC	0810	0958	XX	1258	1446
BSS	0817	1005	XX	1305	1453
BG	0822	1010	XX	1310	1458
GP	0832	1020	XX	1320	1508
LG	0842	1030	XX	1330	1518
LW	0850	1038	XX	1338	1526

Tp.No.	2	4	5	7	9
LW	0904	1052	**	1352	1540
LG	0912	1100	**	1400	1548
GP	0921	1109	**	1409	1557
BNS	0931	1119	1231	1419	1607
BSS	0937	**	1237	1425	1613
BCC	0944	**	1244	1432	1620
LB	XX	XX	XX	XX	XX
FG	XX	XX	XX	XX	XX
GSG	XX	XX	XX	XX	XX
MG	XX	XX	XX	XX	XX

Hand over to Duty 17

Travel on bus 74 (Route 358,Duty 707) 1637BCC-1649MG   **SIGN OFF 1700**

21/11/92

Early morning on 7th July 1993 with a Leyland Olympian about to start its day's work on Duty 20. *Graham Sanders*

revenue earning duties on route 261 bound for Lewisham. It is a bright sunny morning and the roads are clear. The scheduled running time reflects the traffic conditions.

The first 61 will leave the depot at 0525 and the first 358 driver will sign on at 0530. Metrobus makes strenuous efforts to ensure the punctuality of its services and takes a hard line on early running. The controllers will be closely monitoring all routes throughout the day.

Vehicles are neatly parked in the depot area in preparation for the early morning run-out. This 1991 view demonstrates a selection mostly comprising DMSs. *Lyndon Rowe*

The engine of Leyland Olympian J812 GGW receives routine maintenance in the workshop. *Metrobus*

Leyland Tiger H220 JLJ enters the bus-wash after working route 705 from Victoria to Dunton Green. It will then proceed to the parking area. *Metrobus.*

Arriving at Eastbourne Pier on May Day Bank Holiday 1992 ready for the return northwards on Coastlink services 355 and 365 are Olympians J812 and J813 GGW. *Graham Sanders*

AEC Reliance ODV 405W in its latest livery leaves St Olave's school on a regular contract journey. *Graham Sanders*

Metrobus drivers are allocated to one of four rotas covering the 61/261, 146/351, and 353/354/356/357. The fourth rota, route 358, is not shared with any other route. Bus drivers work a basic five-day, forty-five hour week and some overtime is available to boost earnings. Overtime normally arises at short notice due to staff sickness or large coach requirements on a particular day. The longest shifts last about twelve hours, but drivers will not be on the road for that time. Shifts are normally in two parts, with a meal-break in between, and the longest scheduled driving period without a break is five hours seventeen minutes, which is just short of the legal maximum of five hours thirty minutes. Twelve-hour shifts normally occur on 'spreadover', which means that the driver covers both morning and evening peak periods with a long break in the middle of the day. These are a particular feature of the Croydon routes, where the vehicle requirement increases from six to eleven buses at peak times. Drivers' duties vary each day, hence a twelve-hour shift one day may be followed by a much shorter one the following day.

Coach drivers' work is more variable. They usually work for twelve days followed by a four day break. Each coach has its own regular driver, which encourages him to look after the vehicle, although others will obviously take the wheel from time to time.

At 0515 the driver due to report for duty 306 on routes 353/4/6/7 telephones to say he is sick. This duty is due to sign on at 0615, and he is therefore just within the one-hour's notice period required by the Company. Controller Bob Lancaster reorganises two other drivers duties in order to cover this long shift, and finally drafts in spare driver Keith Butler to cover the remaining duty. Keith would otherwise have assisted in the workshop.

Today, the first coach driver is due to sign on at 0550. He is Arthur Hemmens, who came to Metrobus with the takeover of Jason's Coaches. Arthur will take his regular coach, B43 DNY, on an early morning Ministry of Defence contract from Eltham to Fort Halstead. He is due to arrive there at 0750 and will then proceed to Tunbridge Wells, for 0830, to pick up a party for an all-day sightseeing tour of London.

The second coach driver of the day, Shaun Hopps, is close behind. He will take brand new Dennis Javelin K206 GMX to Dunton Green, where he commences a journey on 'Londonlink' route 705 via Biggin Hill to the City of London and Victoria. He is scheduled to leave Victoria at 0915 for Hoverspeed flight 548 at Dover, with passengers bound for Paris and Amsterdam. Shaun will return to London having connected with incoming flight 656 and will then pick up a journey on route 705 to Biggin Hill and Dunton Green, before returning to the depot. This is quite a long day's work and maximises the driver's legal driving period. It is, nevertheless, a typical shift designed to utilise staff and vehicle resources on this type of work to the fullest extent.

By 0600 Director Gary Wood and Controller Andy Toal have arrived. Andy's first job is to reconcile the previous day's revenue. He joins Bob at the counter dealing with drivers' questions as they sign in, and they also deal with visitors. The next two hours will be very busy and by 0810 all 44 scheduled buses, plus 20 coaches will have left the garage. However the telephones and radio are quiet so there are few distractions. Gary checks that everything is running smoothly, both in the office and in the depot. He then opens up his own office, shared with fellow Director Peter Larking who will arrive later. With his door left open, Gary is very much aware of everything going on, and is available to everyone.

At 0635 Driver Norman Pinnegar signs on. Norman is the company's longest-serving driver. He has been with Metrobus since its formation, and prior to that he worked for both Tillingbourne and Orpington & District. Norman has experienced many changes over the years, and clearly enjoys his work. Like Norman, all drivers sign on wearing their uniform of a blue blazer and company tie. The uniform is regarded as an important part of the company image and it is a condition of employment that drivers must be appropriately dressed when on duty. Today's duty for Norman will be 308, a 'spreadover', mostly on route 354, which will not finish until 1930. Norman prefers this to his shorter duty the following day, on rural route 146 which will be "too quiet".

The signing-on area, adjacent to the main office is covered by official notices and regulations regarding the acceptance of passes, fare tables and reminders of correct practices. Drivers are also advised that the old 10p coin ceased being legal tender on 1st July, and must not be accepted. A promotional poster for the 1993 'Bus Driver of the Year' competition is given prominence. Internal heats took place on 27th June, the winners going forward to national finals in Blackpool in September. There are two categories, for full size buses and minibuses (including Dennis Darts) In 1992 Metrobus driver Steve Ellis came twelfth. This was a major achievement for a small company competing against operators with much larger workforces. Controller Bob Lancaster is keen to encourage staff to participate in the competition, which helps to maintain good morale.

At 0700 Assistant Traffic Manager John Hill arrives. John's responsibilities include scheduling the day's coaches to ensure the maximisation of resources. As far as possible, coach duties are combined with other work, such as school runs. In common with other office-based staff, including the Directors, he will help in other areas and will occasionally spend a day driving buses or coaches.

For coach driver Frank Ritchie it is a fairly typical day, and he arrives early for his duty, signing on at 0725. He will leave the depot in coach J201 FMX on a regular local schools run, from nearby Sevenoaks Way to Bullers Wood School in Chislehurst. Afterwards the coach is one of two hired from Metrobus by Sidcup Association for the Blind for a day trip to Eastbourne. It will be returning from Eastbourne at 1730 and, having dropped off its passengers in Sidcup, Frank will return his coach to the depot.

June and July are busy months for private hire work. School outings are at their peak, and foreign language students are to be collected or taken on tours, on top of heavy contract requirements for the Hoverspeed service. The situation eases after the schools break up at the end of July. With resources fully stretched on the coaching side today, it has been

Leyland Tiger J201 FMX waits beneath the white cliffs at Dover, Eastern Docks, before boarding a ferry to Calais. *Graham Sanders*

necessary to transfer some bus drivers to coach duties and to cover bus work on overtime, or by using office staff. Amongst other private hires today, coaches will be visiting Broadstairs, Hever Castle, Gatwick Airport, Chiddingstone, and Streatham Ice Rink. Three coaches will be taking foreign language students on a tour of London's sights, and one will be meeting a party of students from Moscow at Heathrow Airport.

Metrobus operates an extensive 'Daybreak' excursions programme to a variety of destinations and this year a number of weekend 'minibreaks' have been added. During the summer there are tours on most days, but today is an exception. Knowing that Wednesdays are particularly busy for private hire work, Traffic Manager Dave Hunt avoids scheduling excursions on these days, although they will resume the following Wednesday. The excursions are well patronised, with up to three coaches being required for some trips. Charges vary from about £10 to £20 per passenger, depending on distance and whether entry charges to places of interest are included. There are discounts for pensioners and children. Afternoon-only tours are cheaper and foreign or weekend breaks more expensive.

GREAT DAYS OUT WITH

METROBUS

AND
SOUTHLANDS COACHES

NEW FOR '93
WEEKEND
MINIBREAKS

Daybreaks and Summer Services
April - September 1993

Metrobus 'Daybreak' passengers are assisted aboard their coach, Tiger H220 JLJ about to depart Ostend for home on 21st August 1993. *Graham Sanders*

DAF coach E957 GGX waits in the car park at Devils Dyke in Sussex while its passengers enjoy the scenery on a daybreak tour, which also includes a visit to Arundel. *Graham Sanders*

One early morning visitor to the office is from the London Transport Tendered Bus Division, bringing supplies of ticket machine rolls, 'Special Occurrence' forms and 'Tickets Issued in Error' forms, emergency tickets, and depot reader ticket rolls. Data is returned at the same time for delivery to LT's headquarters at 55 Broadway in central London.

Chief Engineer Chris Prowse arrives at 0800 at the start of a nine-hour day. Engineering staff work variable hours according to their job. Depot foremen work a continuous twelve-hour shift for seven days, followed by seven days rest. Others work one of three shorter shifts, between 0500 and 0100 the following morning, or a regular 9-5 pattern. There are currently two Youth Training Scheme trainees employed, which is normal practice. The ratio of skilled to semi-skilled engineering staff is about fifty/fifty. All engineering staff can drive, and may be asked to do so when needed.

At the end of each shift, drivers must report all vehicle faults and these are usually attended to overnight. There is a policy of preventive maintenance to minimise breakdowns which has been very successful, and roadside failures are rare. When they do occur, a spare vehicle is always ready to be despatched as soon as a call is received. Metrobus is justifiably proud of its claim that it never cancels a bus or coach due to vehicle or staff shortages and today is no exception.

Buses require an annual 'FFD' (Freedom From Defect) test, often referred to as an 'MoT', which involves the vehicle travelling to the Mitcham testing station. Chris Prowse prepares a rota covering all buses and coaches. Many of the newer buses have been delivered in batches of up to nine, and it is necessary to spread the requirement evenly across the year so that buses can be sent for their FFD after just six months service. Today, one year old Leyland Olympian K815 HMV will be tested, and engineer Derek Parker will drive it to Mitcham. In preparation for this, it had entered the workshop on Monday to undergo a chassis clean and a thorough interior clean. Dennis Dart J702 EMX is currently over the pits being prepared for its FFD later in the week. Elsewhere, two Roe-bodied Olympians, UWW 14X and CUB 66Y, are receiving routine maintenance and cleaning. This results in the two remaining DMSs, OJD 198R and OJD 243R being used on route 261. Newer buses could have been allocated, but the DMSs are in good condition and they would otherwise be stored until required the following Saturday. Apart from this feature, it is not normal practice to mix vehicle types on routes.

At 0800 there is only one more bus to leave the depot for the morning shift, and the signing-on area has become very quiet. Controller Bob Lancaster decides to go to Bromley North. This is the point where most buses can be seen and it is an effective location from which to regulate services. It is now the height of the morning rush hour and roadworks by British Gas at Keston are delaying buses back to the A21 beyond Locks Bottom. This disrupts not only the Croydon routes but the 61, 261 and 358 too. The 358s are being further delayed by roadworks in Shortlands. The 358 journey from Orpington at 0850 took an hour to reach Bromley South (the scheduled time is 27 minutes). An extra bus is used to restore the headway. In Cameron Road, Bromley, route 354 is affected by cable laying works. Buses on route 61 are also being delayed as a result of roadworks in Chislehurst Road. In general, it is these temporary roadworks which create most problems. Day-to-day peak-hour congestion is largely predictable and the schedules are designed to take account of it. For example, buses on route 261 which can be badly delayed in Bromley and Lewisham, have 14 minutes layover at each end of the route. It would be possible for the service to be operated at the same frequency with one fewer bus and shorter layovers, but the regularity would suffer and mileage would be lost. On route 61 one fewer bus is scheduled in the middle of the day, when the frequency is reduced from 12 to 15 minutes. The spare bus stays at Bromley North station so that it can be used if a gap occurs.

Lost mileage arising from buses turned short of their destination as a result of traffic congestion is not a daily event. Unfortunately Bob Lancaster finds he needs to take such action at 1030 when two 61s arrive at Bromley North together, one being 20 minutes late following traffic hold-ups. The driver of the late-running bus on Duty 24 is due for a meal relief and to avoid sending two buses back to Chislehurst together, Bob decides to dispatch the first one out of service to Masons Hill via Kentish Way relief road rather than Bromley High Street. This will enable it to save several minutes, and Duty 24 should be back on time for the following journey from Chislehurst. This is the first lost mileage since the previous Saturday.

London Transport requires all operators of tendered services to operate at least 98.5% of their scheduled mileage, but does not set targets for mileage lost through traffic congestion. Metrobus aims to run 100% of its scheduled services and regularly achieves 99.9% of its planned mileage. Sometimes, when extra buses are placed in service, the actual mileage operated during the course of a day can exceed 100% of the schedule.

Back at the depot, the driver of Olympian H811 AGX reports a door defect while operating on route 357. It returns to the depot as scheduled, is attended to, and passed fit for further service by midday. At lunchtime, Peter Larking discusses the day's work so far with Chris Prowse in the workshops. Most coaches have now left the depot, but there are about a dozen buses left, either spare, on spreadover duties or being attended to by the engineers. One spreadover vehicle today is the sole double deck coach B688 BPU.

The office is now buzzing with telephone enquiries, handled mostly by Rita Whitehead, the only female member of the administrative staff Rita came to Metrobus in October 1991, having previously worked for Southland Coaches. She deals with coach bookings and general enquiries during normal office hours.

Traffic Manager Dave Hunt arrives at midday and will stay on duty until mid-evening. Dave has worked for Metrobus since its formation, albeit in a part-time capacity at first. He previously worked for National Express and takes a particular interest in the coach side of the business. The *Great Days Out with Metrobus* publication, listing the company's excursion programme is all Dave's work. It includes details of the attractions available at each destination and is packed with suggestions for visitors. This approach has been extremely successful in increasing the number of coach passengers each year. No fewer than 65,000 free 28-page brochures were printed this year. They are distributed inside vehicles, through travel agents and by post.

At 1400, Assistant Traffic Manager John Hill realises that he is short of three drivers for the following day. The shortage has arisen through the need to transfer some bus drivers to coach work to cover heavy commitments. A diary of all drivers who are willing to work on their day off is kept in the office, but unfortunately only one of these is available. The next stage is to pick up the phone and start asking other likely candidates. Controller Andy Toal also rings around. Needless to say, this activity requires a degree of charm and tact, and even then it can be a long drawn-out process.

One of the main reasons for the day-to-day fluctuations on the coaching side is the Hoverspeed City Sprint contract. Hoverspeed send through their basic coach requirements a week at a time but are unable to confirm precise numbers of coaches they require until the day before. They can require up to three coaches to meet each flight, and it can be difficult to find staff (and sometimes coaches) at short notice. Today, a maximum of two coaches is required for any one flight, but requirements are often different in each direction. Hence a coach may leave Victoria on its own, but the return journey from Dover could require three vehicles to carry all pre-booked passengers.

Coach work is generally only profitable in the summer months, and at these times it is essential to utilise the fleet effectively, which requires considerable skill. Although computer software packages are now available for scheduling purposes, there is sufficient human expertise on hand to plan rotas efficiently. Computers are however used for excursion bookings and a variety of other functions.

At 1430 Gary Wood leaves the office for home. Meanwhile, Dave Hunt is on the phone attempting to sort out the problem of a Russian student who mistakenly boarded a Metrobus coach at Heathrow Airport, bound for Orpington, when he should have been on his way to Devon! The mistake only came to light when the coach arrived in Bromley. Fortunately the coach was returning to Heathrow afterwards and Dave arranges for the lost student to be returned to the airport. Hopefully those responsible for the student managed to arrange his journey to Devon without further delay.

The problem of finding three additional drivers for the next day is proving a rather a slow process. Duty 21 on route 261 is still partly uncovered. A driver had been found but he was only able to work the first half of the duty. For a while it looked as though even the second half of the duty would have to be split between two drivers on overtime, but eventually someone came to the rescue and agreed to cover all of the afternoon duties. The task becomes a crusade for Andy Toal, who refuses to go home until it is sorted out, and who still manages to sound enthusiastic at 1800, twelve hours after his arrival.

The evening peak runs smoothly, with all buses running to schedule, and no breakdowns or major hold-ups reported. Both afternoon controllers are driving buses today, so it is just as well things are quiet. In the event of any major problems one of the office staff or the Directors would take control. Peter Larking announces his departure at about 1830, but it is almost an hour before he leaves the premises because the phones suddenly become busy. Outside, he observes a defect on a coach awaiting refuelling and makes arrangements for it to be dealt with.

Buses begin returning to the depot at just before 1800 and for the following 90 minutes or so there is a constant procession of buses and coaches arriving. Upon arrival, all vehicles pull up alongside the fuel pump whereupon they record their mileage to an attendant who refuels them. The driver then leaves his vehicle and Night Foremen Dave Todd and Robin Smith take over. They drive through the automatic washer and park the bus or coach in preparation for the next morning. Not all buses are washed every day, especially in the summer, and the coaches tend to be washed by hand. This is because the automatic washing machine is not quite as effective and the coach fleet must always be in sparkling condition. It is important that the refuelling and washing procedure is not delayed, otherwise there will be a queue of vehicles waiting out in the road, creating an obstruction. Fortunately, everything runs smoothly today. The depot area gradually fills up with buses and the cleaners will then attend to the interiors. Any graffiti will be removed before each bus is allowed out again. Experience has shown that removing it the same day is an effective deterrent, since the vandals will not have the satisfaction of seeing their work again.

At 1930 the flow of buses and coaches entering the depot reduces to a trickle. Inside, the drivers are signing off and handing in their Wayfarer receipts. Some will then venture upstairs to buy a drink from the machine or meet colleagues in the snooker room before going home. Dave Hunt is now in charge and most of the activity is now outside. Any minor repairs to vehicles are undertaken during the evening so that the maximum number of vehicles are available for the following morning.

Bus services begin to run down after 2300, with the last bus scheduled to return at 0053. Two coaches will remain out all night on the Hoverspeed City Sprint service. Tonight, eight vehicles have returned with their drivers reporting minor faults, such as gears slipping, a slight fuel leak and a headlight not working. All of these faults are dealt with by the late running shift or the night foremen and all of the vehicles concerned are available for service the following day.

Development of the Green Street Green Site

The company premises at Oak Farm, Green Street Green were inherited from two previous operators, Tillingbourne (Metropolitan) and Orpington & District. As the name suggests, the earliest record of land use there was as a farm. The original malthouse, attached to the farm, had been erected in 1708. Over a century later, in 1836, a brewery was founded on the site by Fox and Sons. The local reputation of the 'Farnborough Ale' was such that 110 people were engaged there in its production, some of whom were housed in cottages on the site.

In 1909 the brewery was closed and the site eventually passed to the Botton family, fairground operators, whose main base was in Norfolk but who used the site as a winter store and local base for travelling fairs operating in the area. As their requirement for such storage reduced, various areas of the site were let to a variety of small businesses, and it was in this way that one of the original Dutch barns was let to Orpington & District in the early seventies.

Having inherited this building, and some of the land surrounding it, Metrobus set about removing the farmyard image and extending the garage premises onto some of the adjoining land. This was done using a building of concrete portal-frame construction purchased from Continental Pioneer of Richmond, Surrey. Having closed their bus and coach operation in 1984, they had no further use for the building, and work to dismantle and transport it to Orpington commenced. By late 1985 its re-erection was complete; this was adjacent to the original barn, the identity of which was removed by its cladding and marriage to the new structure. The result was a garage building large enough for eight vehicles plus a small office. This was a timely expansion of the garage facilities as there were opportunities for route expansion on the horizon. Indeed, it was only a matter of months before the company was negotiating with the landlords for further land to house a rapidly expanding fleet.

One of the greatest challenges to be faced by the company occurred in 1986, when the site owners announced their intention to sell for the highest possible price. Outline applications were duly made to the Planning Department of Bromley Council to turn the site into a housing estate. The value of the 2.5 acre site was immense at that time and beyond the means of a fledgling bus company. The planning applications were fought by Metrobus, along with a number of their light industrial neighbours. A good many local people were opposed to the change for a variety of reasons; not least that some of the surviving farm buildings dating from the turn of the century were of historic importance.

The original Oak Farm premises prior to rebuilding are shown in this 1984 view of the depot with AEC Reliance ODV 404W. *Metrobus*

After two unsuccessful applications and appeals the housing developers retired defeated and it seemed that the cloud had been lifted. Before long, however, a further planning application was made, to build a Do-It-Yourself superstore on the site, which challenged many of the reasons for the refusal of the previous housing scheme. By this time another two years had elapsed, but in the meantime the financial position of Metrobus had improved to a point where funds for the freehold purchase of the site were available. This put an end to further speculative development proposals and was a major achievement for Metrobus.

These uncertainties had nevertheless forced the Company to consider a move to alternative premises. The location at Green Street Green was, and remains today, well placed for the Company's current operations and any move would have been made reluctantly. The various options considered included the former London Buses garage at Sidcup, but the most serious contender was a Ministry of Defence building on the fringe of Biggin Hill airport, whose only use for many years had been for storing aged 'Green Goddess' fire engines which had last seen daylight during the firemen's strike of 1977. The entire Metrobus fleet could have been housed under cover there although the doorways would have required adapting for full-height double deckers. Other considerations were the slightly remote location of Biggin Hill in relation to the company's main activities and the high cost of garaging the entire fleet under cover. However, next to Oak Farm, it was considered the best of the options available and a tender was submitted to the Ministry of Defence, which was accepted after some delay. The delay proved fortunate, though, because in the interim period the company's offer for the Oak Farm site had been accepted and the move to Biggin Hill was never required.

Having completed the site purchase in May 1988, the company submitted planning applications for a number of improvements. These comprised the levelling and resurfacing of the parking area (including cutting back and retaining the A21 embankment), further extension of the garage buildings and new office accommodation. The other tenants who had survived the uncertainties of the previous two years did not fit into the Company's plans too well, but those who wished to stay were offered new five-year leases on the perimeter of the site. A few, including Jason's coaches, were offered the freehold of their site area subject to the opening of a new entrance adjacent to the cottages, which would not interfere with Metrobus operation. At a time of high land values it was clearly in the company's interest to sell off parts of the site it could not foresee needing, including the two surviving original cottages.

The view in 1993 from Farnborough Hill showing the depot buildings ahead and part of the offices on the right, which include the staff facilities. Iveco G407 DPD nearest the camera has just returned from an early morning contract, with other members of the coach fleet waiting on the fuel bay. *Metrobus*

The acquisition of Southland Coaches in 1991 brought with it two further sites, one in Edison Road in central Bromley and another at Southlands Road near Bromley Common. Both of these premises have been retained, partly for strategic reasons, but also to re-locate one tenant from the Green Street Green site. The purchase of Jason's Coaches in February 1993 has returned to Metrobus ownership the land previously transferred to them in 1988. Following expiry of other leases, Metrobus is again in control of the whole site.

Today, the base still retains some of the farm buildings, which are currently in use as stores. The main vehicle workshop has changed internally over the years, both to meet the requirements of an expanding and more varied fleet, and to enable the installation of more equipment and storage facilities. There are two bays, with engineering stores and staff facilities in between, each of which comprises an inspection pit and set of vehicle hoists plus working areas. A secondary two-bay workshop, intended mainly for coaches, is also available but this is normally only used at busy times. One workshop is in use 24 hours a day, seven days a week, with running repairs and routine checks undertaken without the need to remove a vehicle from use. Only major repairs, monthly servicing and annual 'FFD' preparation require the vehicle to be categorised as 'off-road'. A bus-wash bay and chassis cleaning bay are both located externally, and vehicles are parked externally in surfaced and floodlit areas. A purpose-built two-storey building, adjacent to the Farnborough Hill boundary, houses the offices and other staff facilities. This was completed in 1989.

Depot overhead costs are minimised by the use of large uncovered areas for bus and coach parking. Close proximity to all the Company's bus routes and to the motorway network with the M25 providing easy access to the main trunk routes, makes the location an excellent operating facility.

Some of the motley collection of vehicles acquired from Southland Coaches, shortly after the takeover, at the depot. Many of these were disposed of within a few days of their acquisition. The Metrobus AEC Reliance is also present in this view. *Graham Sanders*

Vehicles operated by Metrobus 1983-1993

Bodywork Layout notes:

The first letter denotes the basic type of vehicle - B = single deck bus with bus seats, DP = dual purpose single decker suitable for bus or coach use (but excluding buses fitted with high backed seats). H = Highbridge double decker (14'2" or 14'6" high),

LD = Lowheight double decker (13'8" or 13'10" high). C = coach, CH = Double deck coach.

The numbers indicate seating capacity, the upper deck first (if appropriate) followed by the lower deck seating capacity after the oblique.

The final letter indicates the door layout - F = front entrance/exit, D = front entrance, centre exit. A 't' after the final letter indicates that the vehicle is fitted with a toilet.

Section A - Vehicles no longer in stock

Registration	Chassis	Bodywork	Layout	Previous owner	Arrived	Sold
BYG 851H	Bristol VRTSLG	ECW	LD39/31F	Tillingbourne	9/83	12/84
SPA 192R	Bedford YMT	Plaxton	DP53F	Tillingbourne	9/83	10/84
XPL 889T	Bedford YMT	Duple	B61F	Tillingbourne	9/83	9/86
JTM 109V	AEC Reliance 6U2R	Duple	B53F	Tillingbourne	9/83	9/85
ODV 404W	AEC Reliance 6U2R	Duple	DP53F	Tillingbourne	9/83	12/90
BHL 609K	Daimler Fleetline CRG6LX	Northern Counties	LD43/33F	West Riding	8/84	10/87
BHL 624K	Daimler Fleetline CRG6LX	Northern Counties	LD43/33F	West Riding	8/84	7/87
JPA 140K	AEC Reliance 6U2R	Park Royal	DP47F	Ravensbourne Coaches	9/84	7/85
JPA 154K	AEC Reliance 6U2R	Park Royal	DP47F	Ravensbourne Coaches	9/84	5/85
WKE 67S	Bedford YMT	Duple	B61F	Maidstone Boro' Council	2/85	6/89
BNO 701T	Bedford YMT	Duple	DP53F	Eastern National	3/85	11/86
KUC 898P	Daimler Fleetline CRL6	MCW	H45/25D	London Buses	7/86	7/92
KUC 922P	Daimler Fleetline CRL6	MCW	H45/25D	London Buses	7/86	12/92
KUC 960P	Daimler Fleetline CRL6	MCW	H45/25D	London Buses	7/86	7/92
KUC 977P	Leyland Fleetline FE30ALR	MCW	H45/25D	London Buses	7/86	12/92
OUC 52R	Leyland Fleetline FE30AGR	MCW	H45/25D	London Buses	7/86	12/92
OUC 54R	Leyland Fleetline FE30AGR	MCW	H45/25D	London Buses	7/86	2/91
OUC 56R	Leyland Fleetline FE30AGR	MCW	H45/25D	London Buses	7/86	12/92
OJD 167R	Leyland Fleetline FE30AGR	MCW	H45/25D	London Buses	7/86	11/92
OJD 173R	Leyland Fleetline FE30AGR	MCW	H45/25D	London Buses	7/86	2/91
OJD 200R	Leyland Fleetline FE30AGR	MCW	H45/25D	London Buses	7/86	2/93
OJD 211R	Leyland Fleetline FE30AGR	MCW	H45/25D	London Buses	7/86	12/92
D21 CTR	Bedford YMT	Wadham Stringer	B53F	New	8/86	2/91
D22 CTR	Bedford YMT	Wadham Stringer	B53F	New	8/86	9/90
D23 CTR	Bedford YMT	Wadham Stringer	B53F	New	8/86	2/91
AKK 171T	Bedford YMT	Duple	B61F	Maidstone Boro' Council	8/86	6/89
MKP 181W	Bedford YMT	Wadham Stringer	B61F	Maidstone Boro' Council	11/86	9/87
Q856 MEV	Leyland Leopard PSU3A/4R	Berkhof	DP53F	Southend Trans. (loan)	6/87	10/87
UWW 16X	Leyland Olympian ONLXB/1R	Roe	H47/29F	West Yorkshire PTE	8/87	9/88

F121 TRU	Mercedes-Benz 709D	Reeve Burgess	B25F	New		8/88	1/90
F122 TRU	Mercedes-Benz 709D	Reeve Burgess	B25F	New		8/88	1/90
F123 TRU	Mercedes-Benz 709D	Reeve Burgess	B25F	New		8/88	8/91
F124 TRU	Mercedes-Benz 709D	Reeve Burgess	B25F	New		8/88	1/90
F125 TRU	Mercedes-Benz 709D	Reeve Burgess	B25F	New		8/88	8/91
F126 TRU	Mercedes-Benz 709D	Reeve Burgess	B25F	New		8/88	8/91
F127 TRU	Mercedes-Benz 709D	Reeve Burgess	B25F	New		8/88	1/90
F128 TRU	Mercedes-Benz 709D	Reeve Burgess	B25F	New		8/88	8/91
B43 DNY	Bedford YNT	Duple Laser	C53F	Southland Coaches		10/91	9/93
B47 DNY	Bedford YNT	Duple Laser	C53F	Southland Coaches		10/91	9/93
GDY 500X	Bedford YNT	Plaxton Supreme V	C53F	Southland Coaches		10/91	9/93

Demonstrators operated by Metrobus 1983 - 1993

Registration	Chassis	Bodywork	Date Operated	Routes operated
B263 AMG	Leyland Tiger	Plaxton Paramount 3500	12/85	Private hire
E101 VWA	Neoplan	Neoplan	12/87	353/357
D634 BBV	Leyland Lynx	Leyland	7/87	61/353/354/357
F100 AKB	Renault	Northern Counties	3/89	353/357/361
F756 NPJ	Dennis Javelin	Duple	12/88	357
F370 BUA	Optare Delta	Optare	2/89	353/357
F976 WEF	CVE Omni	Omni	7/89	A/B/C
H398 SYG	Optare Metrorider	Optare	3/91	351
H840 NOC	Dennis Dart	Carlyle	1&2/91	356
H908 DTP	Dennis Dart	Wadham Stringer Portsdown	4/91	356
H737 THL	Renault midibus	Whittaker	3/91	not operated in service
H108 THE	Dennis Dart	Reeve Burgess Pointer	7/91	not operated in service
J648 XHL	Dennis Dart	Reeve Burgess Pointer	9/91	356
J227 DKX	Iveco Turbo City 100	Alexander double deck	5/92	261
J564 URW	Leyland Lynx Mk 2	Leyland	7/92	354/357/361
L733 CKP	Mercedes 609D	Crystals	10 & 11/93	Private hire

All of the above vehicles were single deckers with the exception of Iveco J227 DKX
Other vehicles have been loaned from time to time to cover specific requirements such as rail replacement services.

The following coaches were acquired from Southland Coaches and taken into stock for a short period in October/November 1991.

PRO 446W	Bedford YMQ	Duple	C35F
HMY 972V	Ford	Duple	C53F
FLJ 74V	Ford	Plaxton	C53F
DHE 674V	Ford	Plaxton	C53F
FCW 75W	Ford	Duple	C53F
LTG 277X	Ford	Plaxton	C53F

The following vehicles were hired from Kirkby (the dealer) during April and May 1993 pending the arrival of new coaches for the Hoverspeed service:-

H901 AHS	Volvo B10M-60	Plaxton Paramount	C49Ft
H904 AHS	Volvo B10M-60	Plaxton Paramount	C49Ft
H905 AHS	Volvo B10M-60	Plaxton Paramount	C49Ft
H906 AHS	Volvo B10M-60	Plaxton Paramount	C49Ft

Section B - Fleet as at September 1993

Metrobus vehicles do not carry fleet numbers and are identified by their registration numbers, none of which are duplicated. Since 1989 all *new* buses and coaches have been registered as follows:-

| 101 + Full size single deckers | 701 + Small single deckers |
| 201 + Coaches | 801 + Double deckers |

Registration	Chassis	Bodywork	Layout	Previous owner	Arrived
Buses					
UWW 13X	Leyland Olympian ONLXB/1R	Roe	H47/29F	West Yorkshire PTE	8/87
UWW 14X	Leyland Olympian ONLXB/1R	Roe	H47/29F	West Yorkshire PTE	8/87
CUB 60Y	Leyland Olympian ONLXB/1R	Roe	H47/29F	West Yorkshire PTE	8/87
CUB 61Y	Leyland Olympian ONLXB/1R	Roe	H47/29F	West Yorkshire PTE	8/87
CUB 63Y	Leyland Olympian ONLXB/1R	Roe	H47/29F	West Yorkshire PTE	8/87
CUB 64Y	Leyland Olympian ONLXB/1R	Roe	H47/29F	West Yorkshire PTE	8/87
CUB 66Y	Leyland Olympian ONLXB/1R	Roe	H47/29F	West Yorkshire PTE	8/87
CUB 68Y	Leyland Olympian ONLXB/1R	Roe	H47/29F	West Yorkshire PTE	8/87
CUB 69Y	Leyland Olympian ONLXB/1R	Roe	H47/29F	West Yorkshire PTE	8/87
CUB 71Y	Leyland Olympian ONLXB/1R	Roe	H47/29F	West Yorkshire PTE	8/87
F80 SMC	Leyland Lynx LX112L10ZR1	Leyland	B49F	New	9/88
K101 JMV	Leyland Lynx LX2R11V18Z43	Leyland	B51F	New	8/92
D103 NDW	Leyland Lynx LX112TL11ZR1	Leyland	B51F	Merthyr Tydfil	11/89
D104 NDW	Leyland Lynx LX112TL11ZR1	Leyland	B51F	Merthyr Tydfil	11/89
D110 NDW	Leyland Lynx LX112TL11ZR1	Leyland	B51F	Merthyr Tydfil	11/89
F165 SMT	Leyland Lynx LX112L10ZR1	Leyland	B51F	Miller, Foxton	2/91
F166 SMT	Leyland Lynx LX112L10ZR1	Leyland	B51F	Miller, Foxton	2/91
OJD 198R	Leyland Fleetline FE30AGR	MCW	H45/25D	London Buses	7/86
OJD 243R	Leyland Fleetline FE30AGR	MCW	H45/25D	London Buses	7/86
C395 DML	Leyland Olympian ONLXB/1R	ECW	LD45/32F	New	7/85
XWY 475X	Leyland Olympian ONLXB/1R	ECW	LD45/32F	West Riding	6/87
XWY 476X	Leyland Olympian ONLXB/1R	ECW	LD45/32F	West Riding	6/87
J701 EMX	Dennis Dart 8.5SDL	Plaxton Pointer	B32F	New	8/91
J702 EMX	Dennis Dart 8.5SDL	Plaxton Pointer	B32F	New	8/91
J703 EMX	Dennis Dart 8.5SDL	Plaxton Pointer	B32F	New	8/91
J704 EMX	Dennis Dart 8.5SDL	Plaxton Pointer	B32F	New	8/91
J705 EMX	Dennis Dart 8.5SDL	Plaxton Pointer	B32F	New	8/91
J706 EMX	Dennis Dart 8.5SDL	Plaxton Pointer	B32F	New	8/91
J707 EMX	Dennis Dart 8.5SDL	Plaxton Pointer	B32F	New	8/91
K708 KGU	Dennis Dart 9SDL	Plaxton Pointer	B35F	New	11/92
K709 KGU	Dennis Dart 9SDL	Plaxton Pointer	B35F	New	11/92
K710 KGU	Dennis Dart 9SDL	Plaxton Pointer	B35F	New	11/92
K711 KGU	Dennis Dart 9SDL	Plaxton Pointer	B35F	New	11/92
K712 KGU	Dennis Dart 9SDL	Plaxton Pointer	B35F	New	11/92
K713 KGU	Dennis Dart 9SDL	Plaxton Pointer	B35F	New	11/92
K714 KGU	Dennis Dart 9SDL	Plaxton Pointer	B35F	New	11/92
K715 KGU	Dennis Dart 9SDL	Plaxton Pointer	B35F	New	11/92
K716 KGU	Dennis Dart 9SDL	Plaxton Pointer	B35F	New	11/92

F802 NGU	Leyland Olympian ONCL10/1RZ	Leyland	LD47/31F	New	5/89
F803 NGU	Leyland Olympian ONCL10/1RZ	Leyland	LD47/31F	New	5/89
G804 SMV	Leyland Olympian ON2R50C13Z4	Leyland	LD47/31F	New	2/90
G805 SMV	Leyland Olympian ON2R50C13Z4	Leyland	LD47/31F	New	2/90
G806 TMX	Leyland Olympian ON2R50C13Z4	Leyland	LD47/31F	New	5/90
H807 XMY	Leyland Olympian ON2R50C13Z4	Leyland	LD47/31F	New	5/90
H808 AGX	Leyland Olympian ON2R50C13Z4	Leyland	LD47/31F	New	2/91
H809 AGX	Leyland Olympian ON2R50C13Z4	Leyland	LD47/31F	New	2/91
H810 AGX	Leyland Olympian ON2R50C13Z4	Leyland	LD47/31F	New	2/91
H811 AGX	Leyland Olympian ON2R50C13Z4	Leyland	LD47/31F	New	3/91
J812 GGW	Leyland Olympian ON2R50C13Z4	Leyland	LD47/31F	New	1/92
J813 GGW	Leyland Olympian ON2R50C13Z4	Leyland	LD47/31F	New	1/92
K814 HMV	Leyland Olympian ON2R50C13Z4	Leyland	H47/31F	New	7/92
K815 HMV	Leyland Olympian ON2R50C13Z4	Leyland	H47/31F	New	7/92
K816 HMV	Leyland Olympian ON2R50C13Z4	Leyland	H47/31F	New	7/92

Staff Bus

E575 FTW	Ford Transit	Ford	B11F	Stormont	1/90

Coaches

J51 SNY	Leyland Tiger TRCL10/3ARZM	Plaxton 321	C53F	Bebb, Pontypridd	9/93
J52 SNY	Leyland Tiger TRCL10/3ARZM	Plaxton 321	C53F	Bebb, Pontypridd	9/93
J201 FMX	Leyland Tiger TRCL10/3ARZM	Plaxton 321	C53F	New	10/91
J202 FMX	Leyland Tiger TRCL10/3ARZM	Plaxton 321	C53F	New	10/91
H220 JLJ	Leyland Tiger TRCL10/3ARZA	Plaxton 321	C57F	New	10/90
K203 GMX	Dennis Javelin 12SDA2117	Plaxton Premier	C49Ft	New	5/93
K204 GMX	Dennis Javelin 12SDA2117	Plaxton Premier	C49Ft	New	5/93
K205 GMX	Dennis Javelin 12SDA2117	Plaxton Premier	C49Ft	New	5/93
K206 GMX	Dennis Javelin 12SDA2117	Plaxton Premier	C49Ft	New	5/93
ODV 405W	AEC Reliance 6U2R	Duple	DP53F	Tillingbourne	9/83
G407 DPD	Iveco	Carlyle	DP25F	Tilllingbourne	4/92
G426 YAY	Dennis Javelin 125DA1907	Duple 320	C53Ft	Jason's Coaches	2/93
G427 YAY	Dennis Javelin 125DA1907	Duple 320	C53Ft	Jason's Coaches	2/93
G428 YAY	Dennis Javelin 125DA1907	Duple 320	C53Ft	Jason's Coaches	2/93
G429 YAY	Dennis Javelin 125DA1907	Duple 320	C53Ft	Jason's Coaches	2/93
E597 LVH	DAF MB230 DKVL615	Duple 320	C57F	KF Cars, Gatwick	8/91
E957 GGX	DAF MB230 DKVL615	Duple 320	C57F	New	5/88
ANA 433Y	DAF MB200DKFL600	Plaxton Paramount	C53F	Southland Coaches	10/91
ANA 434Y	DAF MB200DKFL600	Plaxton Paramount	C53F	Southland Coaches	10/91
B688 BPU	Leyland Olympian ONTL11/2R5P	ECW	CH45/28F	Thamesway	5/91

Vehicles in stock, September 1993 (total 74):

Double deck buses	30
Single deck buses	23
Coaches	20
Staff bus	1

Routes Operated by Metrobus, 1983-1993

61 16.08.86 Bromley North Station to Chislehurst via Orpington, daily, extended Sundays to Eltham Station. Taken over from London Buses on LT contract.

19.01.91 Sunday service between Chislehurst and Eltham withdrawn.

146 10.08.91 Bromley North Station to Downe via Hayes. LT contract taken over from Crystals Coaches. Mondays to Saturdays.

208 26.12.90 Special Boxing Day service Orpington to Catford via Petts Wood. LT contract, operated for one day only.

211 26.12.92 Special Boxing Day service, Sidcup, Queen Mary's Hospital to Bromley North via Orpington, Petts Wood. LT contract, operated for one day only.

261 21.11.87 Lewisham to Bromley Common, Crown via Grove Park and Bromley. Taken over from London Buses on LT contract. Daily.

13.05.89 Most Monday to Saturday garage journeys extended from Bromley Common to Green Street Green in service, replacing route 361 journeys. One journey back-projected to Pratts Bottom. Hourly Saturday shopping hours service, Lewisham to Green Street Green.

14.11.92 Last day of Saturday shopping hours service between Lewisham and Green Street Green (replaced by alterations to route 358).

350 24.09.83 Orpington to Brighton. Seasonal Service, acquired from Tillingbourne (Metropolitan). Sundays, and bank holidays, May to September, also Tuesdays and Thursdays during August.

05.05.84 Operation from Fieldway Estate, New Addington withdrawn. Extended from Brighton to Worthing.

06.05.90 Re-routed via Whyteleafe and M25 instead of Purley and Coulsdon.

351 02.03.91 New route. Bromley North Station to Penge via Ravensbourne, Beckenham, Birkbeck and Anerley.

10.08.91 Re-routed at Anerley to serve Anerley Park instead of Oakfield Road.

21.11.92 Re-routed via Bromley, Market Square in both directions.

353 24.09.83 Croydon to Orpington direct via Addington. Acquired from Tillingbourne (Metropolitan). Monday to Friday peaks only.

354 24.09.83 Sanderstead to Bromley, Churchill Theatre via Forestdale, New Addington and Bourne Vale. Mondays to Fridays only. Acquired from Tillingbourne (Metropolitan).

24.10.83 Revised to operate from Croydon via Route 357 to Forestdale, then Coney Hall, Bourne Vale and Bromley. New Addington section withdrawn.

16.08.86 Revised to operate from Bromley North Station to Selsdon, Farley Road via Forestdale.

31.10.87 Re-routed via Selsdon Vale and extended from Selsdon to Croydon (Fairfield Halls) via Croham Road.

13.05.89 Saturday service introduced.

355 24.09.83 Croydon to Forestdale via Coombe Lane. Acquired from Tillingbourne (Metropolitan). Monday to Friday peaks only.

16.08.86 Route number withdrawn. All journeys renumbered 357.

01.05.88 New seasonal service. Lewisham to Hastings, Eastbourne or Thorpe Park. Sundays and bank holidays, May to September (also Wednesdays during August).

07.05.89 Thorpe Park service replaced by additional Hastings service.

06.05.90 Re-routed via Tunbridge Wells.

03.05.92 Seasonal service revised to operate additionally on Fridays during August.

356 26.03.90 New service. Biggin Hill to Croydon via Keston, Coney Hall and West Wickham. Mondays to Saturdays. Garage journeys extended to/from Dunton Green. One Saturday journey in each direction extended to Sevenoaks.

03.09.90 All journeys withdrawn south of Biggin Hill.

31.08.91 Extended from Biggin Hill to Tatsfield Village via Ricketts Hill Road. One journey re-routed via Selsdon instead of West Wickham.

357 24.09.83 Croydon to Orpington via Forestdale. Acquired from Tillingbourne (Metropolitan). Mondays to Saturdays.

12.05.84 Certain journeys extended to Hewitts Farm.

01.09.84 Last day of Hewitts Farm extension.

16.08.86 Former route 355 short-working journeys added.

27.04.91 Sunday service introduced.

358 15.05.89 New route. Crystal Palace to Green Street Green via Beckenham, Bromley and Orpington. Monday to Friday only.

26.03.90 Increased service. Re-routed to serve Anerley and Eden Park.

27.04.91 Saturday service introduced between Crystal Palace and Locks Bottom.

21.11.92 Revised to operate Orpington Station to Crystal Palace via Green Street Green, Farnborough, Bromley High Street, Shortlands, Eden Park and Beckenham. Replaced 361 and former Kentish Bus 471. Sunday service introduced.

361 16.08.86 Bromley North Station to Green Street Green via Farnborough. Taken over from London Buses on LT contract. Mondays to Saturdays.

01.09.87 One Monday to Friday journey extended to Pratts Bottom.

13.05.89 Reduced to operate Monday to Friday shopping hours only. Replaced at other times by extension of 261.

21.11.92 Withdrawn. Replaced by 358.

365 05.05.91 New seasonal service. Crystal Palace to Hastings or Eastbourne via Beckenham and Hayes. Sundays and bank holidays, May to September, also Fridays during August.

03.05.92 Re-routed via Shirley and West Wickham. Introduced on Wednesdays during August.

404 07.04.90 Sevenoaks to Ide Hill. Kent County Council contract, Saturdays.

01.09.90 Last day of operation. Contract passed to Kentish Bus.

493 17.08.91 Orpington Station and Ramsden Estate. Sunday journeys introduced to supplement existing London & Country service.

705 01.06.88 Biggin Hill to Victoria via Bromley, Lewisham and London Bridge. Acquired from Interland Coaches. Monday to Friday peak hours.

25.03.90 Sunday service introduced, Sevenoaks to Victoria via Tower instead of Cannon Street.

23.09.90 Sunday service withdrawn.

21.04.92 All journeys extended to Dunton Green.

Two Fleetlines remained in the fleet in September 1993. One of these, OJD 198R unloads at Locks Bottom on 27th April 1991, the first day of Saturday operation on route 358 and before conversion of the route to single-deck operation. *Graham Sanders*

739 16.04.89 Victoria to Brands Hatch. Special service, race days only.
25.03.90 Revised to operate Victoria to Chartwell via Brands Hatch and Sevenoaks. Sundays and bank holidays.
23.09.90 Service withdrawn.

A 20.08.88 New route. Hever Court to Northfleet via Gravesend. Monday to Saturday.
14.11.88 Extended from Northfleet to Swanscombe.
04.12.88 Sunday service introduced, Gravesend to Swanscombe.
08.04.89 Extended from Hever Court to Singlewell Village. Withdrawn on Sundays.
31.12.89 Last day of operation. Transferred to Kentish Bus.

B 20.08.88 New route. Hever Court to Painters Ash via Gravesend. Monday to Saturday.
14.11.88 Diverted to Painters Ash to serve Coldharbour.
04.12.88 Sunday service introduced, Gravesend to Painters Ash.
08.04.89 Withdrawn between Hever Court and Livingstone Road and diverted to Kings Farm. Withdrawn on Sundays.
31.12.89 Last day of operation. Transferred to Kentish Bus.

C 09.04.89 New route Kings Farm to Swanscombe via Denton, Gravesend, Perry Street and Northfleet. Sundays only.
29.10.89 Last day of operation.

Route 739 was not a major success and did not operate after the 1990 season. Leyland Lynx F80 SMC passes through Swanley. *Graham Sanders*

Route 358 passes the depot, which conveniently enables drivers to change over at that point. Dennis Dart K713 KGU prepares to continue its journey to Orpington. *Graham Sanders*